Houghton Mifflin
Math
Michigan

MEAP
Daily Test Prep
Book

GRADE
4

Program Authors and Reviewers

Authors

Dr. Carole Greenes
Dr. Matt Larson
Dr. Miriam A. Leiva
Dr. Jean M. Shaw
Dr. Lee Stiff
Dr. Bruce R. Vogeli
Dr. Karol Yeatts

Consultants

Dr. Liping Ma, Strategic Consultant
Dr. David Chard, Language and Vocabulary Consultant

Michigan Test Prep Reviewers

Ms. Gabriella Meyers
Duncan Elementary School
Shelby Township, Michigan

Ms. Linda Maison
Duncan Elementary
Macomb, Michigan

Contents

What Is the *MEAP Daily Test Prep Book*?

The *MEAP Daily Test Prep Book* is a 28-week test prep program designed to help teachers prepare students for the Michigan state tests. Houghton Mifflin has designed the program for flexible use in the classroom. The test items in this book provide opportunities for assessing the content of *Houghton Mifflin Math* while offering test items that reflect the types of questions found in the MEAP tests. Each week of the program presents ten test items, five in Guided Practice format, five in MEAP test format. For each group of five items, there are four multiple-choice items and one constructed-response item.

The first three weeks of the book review students' knowledge of the previous grade level's math content. Following the three-week review, each week of the *MEAP Daily Test Prep Book* corresponds to a chapter in *Houghton Mifflin Math*. The program concludes with a review of the current year's math content. All items correspond to the Michigan grade-level content expectations for that grade.

Why Is the *MEAP Daily Test Prep Book* an Important Teaching Tool?

The *No Child Left Behind Act* requires states to document that all students are showing academic growth with respect to state standards. Assessing student progress in mathematics is no exception. States are now required to regularly assess student performance in achieving specified objectives in mathematics. Houghton Mifflin's *MEAP Daily Test Prep Book* helps teachers monitor and assess student progress over the course of the school year. It also helps build student confidence in taking tests.

Using the *MEAP Daily Test Prep Book*

The *MEAP Daily Test Prep Book* gives teachers the flexibility to incorporate test prep into the classroom on a daily or weekly basis. Each week of the program includes ten test items. Depending on instruction time available and the needs of students, you may want to use the four Guided Practice multiple-choice items one day, followed the next day by the four MEAP Practice Test multiple-choice items. Then you could use the Guided Practice constructed-response item on another day, discuss the answers, and give the Practice Test constructed-response item a day after that. Or you may choose to do everything on one day.

Evaluating Student Performance

Answer keys are provided in the back of the book for all items in the *MEAP Daily Test Prep Book*. Item-specific rubrics are provided for each constructed response question.

Test-Taking Tips

You may wish to offer students the following advice for doing well on tests.

Tell students what to expect on the test. Explain that some test questions will include pictures, graphs, and tables. Point out that it is important to look carefully at information given with each question before answering it. Familiarize students with the organization of the test and the format of the test items.

- Tell students that the test questions are either in a multiple-choice or in an open-ended format.

- Show students how to darken a bubble for their answer. Remind students that only one answer bubble should be filled in for each question.

Strategies for Answering Multiple-Choice Questions

- Encourage students to carefully read each question.

- Remind students to look at all the answer choices before selecting an answer.

- Emphasize that there is only one correct answer.

- If students are not sure how to answer a question, encourage them to go on to the next one.

- Suggest that students try to answer all questions rather than leave a question blank. Encourage educated guessing rather than leaving a question blank.

- Remind students to be careful to fill in the correct space for the answer they want.

Strategies for Answering Constructed-Response Questions

- Point out to students that for the last question in each test they will solve problems and write about how they solved them. Explain that they can write their answers on the same sheet as the problems.

- Tell students to read the problem once to be sure it makes sense to them. They should reread the problem to look for information they need. Encourage them to try to picture the situation and predict what information is needed. In some cases, making a drawing can help.

- Tell students to estimate whenever possible before solving a problem. They should use estimates to check that their answers are reasonable.

- If students can't give a complete answer, encourage them to show what they do know. Explain that they may receive some points for part of an answer.

Before the Test Begins

- Preparation is the key to having students do well on any standardized tests. Explain the importance of preparing for tests by making sure to get enough sleep the night before the test and to eat a good breakfast that morning.

At the End of the Test

- Remind students to check their tests to make sure that every question has been answered and that one answer bubble has been filled in for each multiple-choice question.

MEAP Guided Practice

1 What is the place value of 3 in 83,492?

    A 3 is in the ten thousands place.
    B 3 is in the thousands place.
    C 3 is in the hundreds place.
    D 3 is in the tens place.

Selected Response

Ask Yourself

What is the value of each digit in the number?

TEST TIPS

---

2 Ana has 148 basketball cards in her collection. Travis has 127 basketball cards. What is the best estimate of how many cards they have in all?

    A 180
    B 220
    C 280
    D 300

Selected Response

Ask Yourself

Can I use rounding to estimate?

TEST TIPS

Go On

3 The theater in the history museum can seat 205 students. So far, 87 girls and 79 boys are seated in the theater. How many seats are still empty?

A 39
B 49
C 139
D 166

Selected Response

Ask Yourself

Which operations should I use to solve the problem?

4 Stan buys 8 pencils. Each pencil costs $0.25. Which of the following groups of coins can Stan use to pay for the pencils?

A 8 dimes
B 8 nickels
C 16 dimes
D 4 quarters and 10 dimes

Selected Response

Ask Yourself

What is the value of each group of coins?

Go On

5   Ms. Flores conducted a survey of her students to find out how many books they read during the summer. The bar graph below shows the results of her survey.

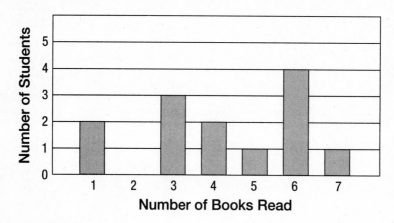

How many students read fewer than 6 books?

What is the range of the data?

Explain your thinking.

Constructed Response

Ask Yourself

What does the height of each bar show?

TEST TIPS

Stop

Name _____   Date _____

1 Which set of numbers can be written as a
multiplication fact family?

  A 5, 8, 13
  B 4, 8, 12
  C 4, 6, 24
  D 4, 6, 10

Selected Response

Ask Yourself

How is multiplication
related to division?

TEST
TIPS

---

2 Which is the **best** estimate for the weight of a
watermelon?

  A   2 ounces
  B   3 liters
  C   12 pounds
  D 2,000 ounces

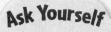

Selected Response

Ask Yourself

Do I need a small
or large unit of
measure?

TEST
TIPS

Go On ▶

3   Sarah plants 9 sunflowers in her garden. She plants 4 times as many daisies. How many more daisies than sunflowers does Sarah plant?

    A 36
    B 27
    C 25
    D 21

Selected Response

Ask Yourself

What steps should I take to solve this problem?

4   The Rashid family visits the Henry Ford Museum in Dearborn, Michigan. The clocks show the time they arrive at the museum and the time they leave the museum.

Arrive   **Leave**

How long are they at the museum?

    A 3 hours 20 minutes
    B 2 hours 30 minutes
    C 2 hours 20 minutes
    D 1 hour 40 minutes

Selected Response

Ask Yourself

At what time do I start counting? Do I need to count hours and minutes?

Go On

5 Chaz is making granola bars for the school bake sale. He wants to put 7 granola bars into each of the six bags.

How many granola bars does Chaz need?

Explain how you got your answer and show all your work.

Chaz decorates the bags by putting 3 stickers on 4 bags and 5 stickers on 2 of the bags.

How many stickers does he need?

Explain your thinking. Show all your work.

Stop

1   Which of the following is another way to write $\frac{5}{8}$?

A $\frac{1}{3} + \frac{3}{4} + \frac{1}{1}$

B $\frac{1}{8} + \frac{1}{8} + \frac{1}{8} + \frac{1}{8} + \frac{1}{8}$

C $\frac{4}{8} + \frac{1}{4}$

D $\frac{3}{2} + \frac{2}{6}$

Selected Response

Ask Yourself

What does a denominator tell? What does a numerator tell?

TEST TIPS

2   Which of the following is the most appropriate for measuring the area of Michigan?

A   centimeters
B   meters
C   square kilometers
D   square inches

Selected Response

Ask Yourself

Am I measuring a large or small area?

TEST TIPS

Go On ➡

Name _____ Date _____

3 Which of these figures does NOT have any parallel sides?

Figure 1   Figure 2   Figure 3   Figure 4

A Figure 1
B Figure 2
C Figure 3
D Figure 4

4 Which fraction stands for the shaded part of the circle?

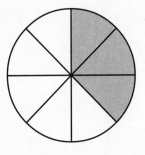

A $\frac{1}{8}$

B $\frac{3}{8}$

C $\frac{5}{8}$

D $\frac{3}{5}$

Go On

5   Mr. Willis is putting a wallpaper border around his living room. The room is 20 feet long and 15 feet wide.

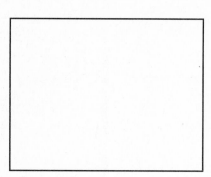

Ask Yourself

Did I label the parallel sides with the same number of feet?

TEST TIPS

Label the length and width of each side on the figure above.

How much wallpaper border does Mr. Willis need to buy?

Explain how you found the answer. Show all your work.

Stop

1 The area of Michigan is about 151,000 square kilometers. What is another way to write 151,000?

A   1 thousand, 51 hundred
B   15 thousand, 1 hundred
C   150 thousand, 1 hundred
D   151 thousand

Selected Response

Ask Yourself

What is the value of each digit in the number?

TEST TIPS

2 Janet is thinking of a number. The digit in the millions place is 8. The digit in the hundreds place is 6 and the digit in the tens place is 5. Which of the following would be Janet's number?

A   807,653
B   865,090
C 8,800,560
D 8,050,650

Selected Response

Ask Yourself

What is the value of each digit in the number?

TEST TIPS

Go On

3 Mount Curwood, the highest point in
Michigan, is about 1,900 feet above sea level.
How many hundreds of feet above sea level is
Mount Curwood?

A   1
B   19
C   190
D 1,900

Selected Response

Ask Yourself

How can I use what
I know about place
value?

4 Ms. Rodriguez divides her class into 4 teams.
She gives each team a problem to solve. The
problem given to each team is shown below.

- Team 1: How many thousands are there in half a million?
- Team 2: How many hundreds are there in half a million?
- Team 3: How many hundreds are there in a hundred thousand?
- Team 4: How many tens are there in ten thousand?

If each team gets the correct answer, for which
team is the answer 5,000?

A Team 1
B Team 2
C Team 3
D Team 4

Selected Response

Ask Yourself

Can I use what
I know about place
value to solve
the problem?

Go On

Constructed Response

5   Juan is playing a game. He picks four number cards. Use the clues below to find what cards he picks.

- Each card has a different number greater than 0 and less than 10.

- Three cards have even numbers.

- The even numbers are all less than the odd number.

- The odd number can only be divided evenly by 1 and by itself.

Explain how you found your answer. Show your work.

Ask Yourself

How does each clue help me find what numbers could be on the cards?

TEST
TIPS

Stop

Name _____   Date _____

1 The table below shows the number of votes
cast in a presidential election in three different
states.

States	Votes
Michigan	4,858,006
Ohio	4,958,592
Wisconsin	4,658,090

Which of the following place values helps
determine the state with the most number of
votes cast?

A hundred thousands
B millions
C ten thousands
D thousands

2 Which number should be written in the box
below to make the number sentence true?

135,498 > ☐

A 136,345
B 135,948
C 135,498
D 135,238

Go On

3   What is the greatest even number that can be created using all the number cards shown below? Each digit can only be used once.

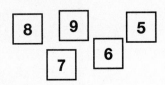

A 98,756
B 98,765
C 97,658
D 97,568

Selected Response

Ask Yourself

How can I use place value to solve the problem?

TEST TIPS

4   Sally, Jacob, Rosa, and Brent cleaned up a park on Saturday. The graph below shows how many cans each person picked up. About how many more cans did Brent pick up than Sally?

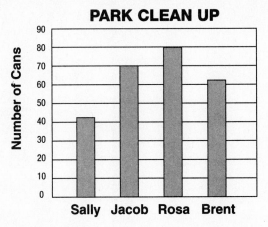

PARK CLEAN UP

A about 30
B about 20
C about 10
D about 5

Selected Response

Ask Yourself

How does the graph show me the information I need?

TEST TIPS

Go On

5 Beth has 5 one-dollar bills and 4 quarters to buy lunch. She wants to order a grilled cheese sandwich, a pasta salad, and lemonade.

Round each menu item Beth wants to the nearest dollar. Does Beth have enough money to buy what she wants?

Lunch Menu

Chicken Sandwich	$4.65
Grilled Cheese	$2.85
Garden Salad	$1.75
Pasta Salad	89¢
Bottled Water	$1.19
Lemonade	99¢

Explain how you found the answer. Show all your work.

Ask Yourself

Do I round up or down?

TEST TIPS

Stop

Name _____ Date _____

1 Deb went shopping at the store sale. She bought 2 caps and a shirt. About how much money did she pay for those three items?

STORE SALE

Gloves	$8.46
Socks	$1.44 pair
Cap	$5.97
Sneakers	$20.99
Sunglasses	$7.82
Shirt	$14.79

A $17
B $27
C $37
D $47

Selected Response

Ask Yourself

To which place am I rounding?

2 The population of Springfield increased by 35,354 between 1990 and 2000. Which of the following sets of numbers represents the population of Springfield in 1990 and 2000?

A Population in 1990: 23,690; Population in 2000: 58,681
B Population in 1990: 23,000; Population in 2000: 59,000
C Population in 1990: 23,327; Population in 2000: 58,681
D Population in 1990: 23,012; Population in 2000: 58,988

Selected Response

Ask Yourself

Do I need an estimate or an exact answer?

Go On

Name _____ Date _____

3 Which of the following can be solved mentally using properties of addition?

    A 83 + 218 + 43
    B 16 + 239 + 48
    C 35 + 209 + 47
    D 93 + 421 + 7

Selected Response

Ask Yourself

Which property makes the calculation easier?

TEST TIPS

4 Music festivals are popular in many places. In Chicago, 21,647 people attended the Ravinia Festival. In Cleveland, 22,496 people attended the Blossom Music Festival. How many more people attended the Cleveland festival than the Chicago festival?

    A 849
    B 949
    C 959
    D 981

Selected Response

Ask Yourself

What steps are needed to solve this problem?

TEST TIPS

Go On

5 Hopkins Elementary School has 872 students.
West Ridge Elementary has 694 students.

How many more students does Hopkins
Elementary School have than West Ridge
Elementary?

Explain how you found the answer. Show your
work.

If 53 students move from Hopkins Elementary
to West Ridge Elementary, how many students
will each school have then?

Explain how you found the answer. Show your
work.

Constructed Response

Ask Yourself

What should I do first
to solve each part of
the problem?

TEST
TIPS

Stop

Name _____ Date _____

1 Lara is training for the marathon. The table below shows her training goals for the first two weeks.

Week	Number of Training Sessions	Total Miles
Week 1	5	50
Week 2	6	72

At the beginning of each week Lara plans her training sessions so that she runs the same distance in each session that week. How many more miles does she run in a training session in the second week than a training session in the first week?

A 22 miles
B 12 miles
C 4 miles
D 2 miles

2 Campers at Camp Lakeview pose for a group photo. 36 campers sit on three benches and 15 campers stand behind the benches. If the three benches seat the same number of campers, how many campers does each bench seat?

A 17
B 12
C 6
D 5

Go On

3 There are 7 students on a camping trip. There are 23 snacks for them to share. Each student gets an equal number of snacks. How many snacks can each student get? How many snacks are left over?

A 2 with 1 left over
B 3 with 2 left over
C 3 with 4 left over
D 4 with 3 left over

Selected Response

Ask Yourself

Is there a remainder? Is it less than the divisor?

TEST TIPS

4 Anya plays a game of ring toss at the school fair and gets a score of 102. She tosses 3 rings into the outer circle, misses one toss, and tosses the rest in the center circle.

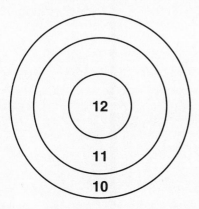

How many tosses did Anya try?

A 4
B 6
C 9
D 10

Selected Response

Ask Yourself

What steps should I take to solve the problem?

TEST TIPS

Go On

5 Kortney's family is moving to a different apartment. The table below shows the items Kortney needs to pack, and the number of each item that she can pack in a box.

Constructed Response

Ask Yourself

Is there a remainder? What do I do with the remainder?

TEST TIPS

Items	Number of items per box
27 dishes	5
40 glasses	7
20 bowls	5
72 books	6

How many boxes will Kortney need?

Explain how you arrived at your answer. Show all your work.

Kortney can use her wagon to take 2 boxes at a time to the moving van. How many trips must she make to take all the boxes to the moving van?

Explain your answer.

Stop

Name _____   Date _____

1 Jonah solves an equation. The solution to the equation is $x = 6$. Which of the following could be the equation Jonah solves?

   A $x + 12 = 6$
   B $x \div 2 = 3$
   C $6x = 12$
   D $2x = 6$

2 Rasha swims 5 times a week with the swim team. She swims 5,000 meters each week, swimming the same distance in each of the 5 training sessions. Which of the following shows the equation she used to find how many meters she swims in each session, and the correct solution to the equation?

   A $a = 5{,}000 \div 5$; 1,000 meters
   B $5a = 5{,}000$; 100 meters
   C $5a = 1{,}000$; 200 meters
   D $a \div 5 = 5{,}000$; 2,500 meters

Go On

3 The solutions to the equations below show Jamie and her brother Oliver's ages. Their sister Nancy's age is the difference between Oliver and Jamie's ages.

Jamie	$a \div 2 = 6$
Oliver	$b \div 2 = 10$

How old is Nancy?

A 8
B 10
C 12
D 20

Selected Response

Ask Yourself

Did I substitute the solution for the variable in the equation to check?

TEST TIPS

4 Yamila, Russell, Ricardo, and LaTanya are playing a game. Each player gets to pick an equation and solve it. The player with the greatest solution advances on the game board.

Yamila	Russell
$a \div 2 = 20$	$a \div 10 = 10$

Ricardo	LaTanya
$2a \div 2 = 20$	$a \div 4 = 20$

Assuming that all four players solve their equation to get the correct solution, who gets to advance on the game board?

A Yamila
B Russell
C Ricardo
D LaTanya

Selected Response

Ask Yourself

What is the value of the variable?

TEST TIPS

Go On

5 Carrie takes 36 photos of birds. She plans to put the photos in an album. Each album page holds 4 photos.

Let *p* stand for the number of pages Carrie needs. Write and solve an equation to find the number of pages she needs.

Explain your thinking and show all your work.

Brooke has 3 times as many photos as Carrie. Each page of her album holds 6 photos. How many album pages does she need?

Explain how you arrived at your answer. Show all your work.

Copyright © Houghton Mifflin Company. All rights reserved.

Constructed Response

Ask Yourself

What facts do I know? How can I use a variable?

TEST TIPS

Stop

1   A bicycle tire makes 8,285 revolutions in one hour. Estimate by rounding. About how many revolutions will a bicycle tire make in 6 hours?

A 25,000 revolutions
B 30,000 revolutions
C 48,000 revolutions
D 60,000 revolutions

Selected Response

Ask Yourself

What does the greater number round to?

2   The Valley Theater is showing a new movie. Each ticket costs $8. The theater's goal is to earn $10,000. If 1,924 people go to the show, how much more than its goal will the theater earn?

A $352
B $1,544
C $3,468
D $5,392

Selected Response

Ask Yourself

Do I need to regroup ones, tens, or hundreds?

Go On

Name _____ Date _____

3 McKenzie would like to earn money by walking her neighbors' dogs. She sees the following posters on a bulletin board.

Walk Trapper!

$2.50 each day
3 days a week

Walk Calvin!

$2.75 each day
4 days a week

How much money would McKenzie earn each week if she takes both jobs?

A $19.50
B $18.50
C $11.00
D $5.25

4 The Dragon, a giant roller coaster, can carry 400 people at one time. Each hour the roller coaster makes 7 trips. If the roller coaster is filled during each trip, how many people can ride it in three hours?

A 1,200
B 2,800
C 8,400
D 8,880

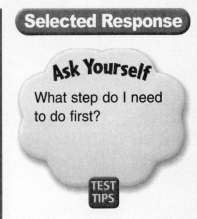

Ask Yourself

What step do I need to do first?

TEST TIPS

Selected Response

Ask Yourself

What basic fact can I use to solve the problem?

TEST TIPS

Go On

5   During the summer, Michael and Sara won 27 ribbons in all for riding their horses at horse shows. Sara won twice as many ribbons as Michael. How many ribbons did they each win?

Explain how you found the answer. Show your work.

Roberto won 8 more ribbons than Michael. Who won more ribbons, Roberto or Sara?

Explain how you arrived at your answer. Show all your work.

Stop

1 Johnson Elementary School buys 18 new computers for its computer lab. If each computer costs $865, about how much did the 18 computers cost?

   A $24,000
   B $22,000
   C $18,000
   D $13,000

Selected Response

Ask Yourself

Can I use rounding to estimate?

TEST TIPS

---

2 There are 40 rooms on each floor of a 50-story hotel. Every day the housekeeping staff leaves 3 towels in each room. How many towels does the housekeeping staff need each day?

   A 200
   B 2,000
   C 6,000
   D 60,000

Selected Response

Ask Yourself

How many zeros should be in the product?

TEST TIPS

3 Callie earns $8.50 each hour working at a restaurant. She works 30 hours each week at the restaurant. Callie also earns $7.50 each hour working at a bookstore. She works 10 hours each week at the bookstore. How much does Callie earn altogether each week?

A $160
B $225
C $255
D $330

Selected Response

Ask Yourself

Which operations should I use to solve the problem?

4 During the last two years, Mr. Wong drove 52 miles round trip each day to work. He worked 238 days in Year 1 and 243 days in Year 2. How many miles did Mr. Wong drive to work during the two years?

A 250,012 miles
B 25,012 miles
C 24,912 miles
D 24,492 miles

Selected Response

Ask Yourself

Which operations should I use to solve the problem?

Go On

5   Ryan is on the school gymnastics team. He and his teammates want to buy 8 T-shirts for the team.

Summer Sale

T-shirts
$6.87

Ryan and his teammates decide to collect cans for recycling. They get a nickel for every can they collect. About how many cans do they need to collect to be able to buy the T-shirts?

Explain how you arrived at your answer. Show all your work.

Ask Yourself

What strategy can I use to tell if my answer is reasonable?

TEST TIPS

Stop

Name _____ Date _____

1 Malick has 8 times as many marbles now as he had a year ago. If Malick has 640 marbles now, how many marbles did he have a year ago?

   A 90
   B 80
   C 72
   D   8

2 Eric's grandparents live in Detroit. Eric lives 350 miles away from them. It takes Eric's mother 7 hours to drive to Detroit. On average how many miles does she drive each hour?

   A   5 miles
   B   7 miles
   C 50 miles
   D 70 miles

Go On

3   Vanessa wants to buy in-line skates that cost $128. She has already saved $63. If she saves $5 each week, how many weeks will it take for her to save enough money to buy the in-line skates?

    A 13
    B 15
    C 18
    D 21

Selected Response

Ask Yourself

What steps should I take to solve the problem?

TEST TIPS

4   Wendy is cutting oranges to bring to her soccer game. She cuts each orange into 4 equal pieces. There are 12 girls on the soccer team. How many oranges does Wendy need to cut so that she will have 6 pieces for each girl?

    A 16
    B 18
    C 22
    D 26

Selected Response

Ask Yourself

How many pieces of orange does Wendy need altogether?

TEST TIPS

Go On

5 Martin Littlefeather makes Native American crafts. He orders 4,400 glass beads and 72 silver beads to make bracelets and necklaces.

If Martin uses 8 silver beads in a necklace, how many necklaces does he make with 72 silver beads? Explain how you got your answer.

If Martin uses 10 glass beads for each bracelet, how many bracelets can he make? Explain how you arrived at your answer. Show all your work.

Show how you can use multiplication to check your answers.

Constructed Response

Ask Yourself
How many zeros should be in the quotient?

TEST TIPS

Stop

Name _____   Date _____

1 Ben, Sarah, and Amanda have a jar with
231 marbles in it. They want to share the
marbles equally. How many marbles will
each receive?

  A 71
  B 76
  C 77
  D 81

Selected Response

Ask Yourself

Can I divide the
hundreds?

TEST
TIPS

2 Mrs. Adams buys 144 hotdogs for a barbeque.
She wants to buy at least 144 hotdog buns to
go with the hotdogs. If the buns come in packs
of 6, 8, or 10, what is the fewest number of
packs that she can buy?

  A 24
  B 18
  C 15
  D 14

Selected Response

Ask Yourself

Can I divide the
hundreds? the tens?
the ones?

TEST
TIPS

Go On

Name _____   Date _____

3   Linda and Harry have a fish farm with three
ponds. They buy 4,800 bass and 3,600 sunfish
to stock the ponds. If they release the same
number of each fish in all three ponds, how
many fish are in each pond?

A 3,800
B 2,800
C 1,600
D 1,200

4   Dominic has 1,271 trading cards. He keeps
the cards in 4 boxes with the same number of
cards in each box. He keeps the leftover cards
on his bookshelf. How many cards are on the
bookshelf?

A 1
B 2
C 3
D 4

Go On

5   A store in Lansing gets a shipment of 848
jeans and 144 shirts. The store manager
arranges all the jeans on 8 shelves. She stacks
the shirts on 6 shelves.

If each shelf holds the same number of jeans,
how many jeans are on each shelf? Explain
how you got your answer and show all your
work.

Assuming that each of the 6 shelves holds the
same number of shirts, how many shirts are
there on each shelf? Explain how you arrived
at your answer.

Show how you can use multiplication to check
your answer.

Constructed Response

Ask Yourself

Can I divide the
hundreds? the tens?
the ones?

TEST
TIPS

Stop

1   Martha correctly listed all the factors of 24.
Which of the following is Martha's list?

A 1, 2, 4, 6, 12, 24
B 1, 2, 3, 4, 6, 12, 24
C 1, 2, 3, 4, 6, 8, 12, 24
D 1, 2, 3, 4, 5, 14, 16, 24

Ask Yourself

How can I find all the factors of a number?

TEST TIPS

2   The picture below shows the shirts for some of
the players on Emilio's soccer team.

Which players have shirts with prime numbers
on them?

A Emilio, Kathy, and Rebecca
B Kathy, Rebecca, and Allen
C Aurelia, Rebecca, and Allen
D Kathy, Aurelia, Allen

Ask Yourself

How many factors does the number have?

TEST TIPS

Go On

3 Celina wrote each factor of 12 on a different card. Then she drew 2 cards. Each card had a prime number. What two cards did she draw?

    A 3, 4

    B 2, 3

    C 1, 12

    D 24, 36

Selected Response

Ask Yourself

What are the factors?

TEST TIPS

4 Jamal is thinking of a number between 10 and 30. The number is a factor of 36 and a multiple of 4. What number is Jamal thinking of?

    A 6

    B 9

    C 12

    D 18

Selected Response

Ask Yourself

Did I find all the factors of 36 between 10 and 30 that are multiples of 4?

TEST TIPS

Go On

5   Raul says that a number that has 10 as a factor will also have 5 as a factor. Is he right?

Explain how you arrived at your answer. Show all your work.

Ask Yourself

What are some numbers that have 10 as a factor?

TEST TIPS

Stop

1   The County Agricultural School raises chickens for sale. The school has 4,460 chickens. The school keeps 860 chickens in a large henhouse and separates the rest of the chickens in 10 coops. If each of the coops holds the same number of chickens, how many chickens are there in each coop?

A 860
B 446
C 360
D 340

Selected Response

Ask Yourself

Which operations should I use to solve the problem?

TEST TIPS

2   Mr. Diaz has a collection of 1,680 stamps. He keeps them in 8 albums. Each album has the same number of stamps. Each album has 10 pages and each page holds the same number of stamps. How many stamps does each page have?

A   20
B   21
C 144
D 168

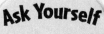Selected Response

Ask Yourself

How do I check my answer?

TEST TIPS

Go On

3 The game warden at a national park counts 4,650 pairs of adult seabirds. Each adult pair raises 4 chicks on average during the breeding season. About how many chicks will be raised at the national park during the season?

A 16,600
B 18,800
C 22,800
D 24,000

4 A group of volunteers works 3 days to build a playground. They work for 6 hours each day. They work a total of 756 hours. How many volunteers are there?

A   36
B   42
C 180
D 420

Go On

5 A family of 2 adults and 3 children visits the Children's Museum on Community Day. They pay a total of $20 for admission.

Ask Yourself

What steps do I take to solve this problem?

TEST TIPS

Community Day
at
Children's Museum

SPECIAL ADMISSION

Children: $2 each

How much is an adult admission? Explain how you found your answer. Show all your work.

On Community Day, how many children could accompany 4 adults for $36? Explain how you arrived at your answer and show all your work.

Stop

1   Daniel is 4 feet 9 inches tall. How many inches tall is he?

A   45 inches
B   48 inches
C   57 inches
D   112 inches

Ask Yourself

How many inches are there in 1 foot?

TEST TIPS

---

2   Which unit is appropriate for measuring how much juice the pitcher shown below can hold?

A   degrees Celsius
B   grams
C   liters
D   meters

Ask Yourself

Am I measuring distance, capacity, or mass?

TEST TIPS

Go On

3 Felicia needs 20 ounces of flour to bake a cake. The store only sells 1 lb, 2 lb, 4 lb, and 10 lb bags of flour. What is the smallest bag Felicia can buy so that she has enough flour for the cake?

A 1 lb bag
B 2 lb bag
C 4 lb bag
D 10 lb bag

Selected Response

Ask Yourself

Am I converting to a larger or smaller unit?

TEST
TIPS

4 Use your ruler to help you solve this problem.

Suki uses the piece of ribbon shown below to make a bow. She uses 100 bows of the same size to decorate a craft project. How many meters of ribbon does Suki need to make all the bows?

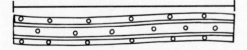

A $2\frac{1}{2}$ meters
B 6 meters
C 10 meters
D 60 meters

Selected Response

Ask Yourself

Did I line up the end of the ribbon with the left end of the ruler?

TEST
TIPS

Go On

5   Laney wants to replace the glass in the living room window. The height of the window is 1.35 meters. At the store, Laney decides to round the height to the nearest meter and buys the glass using that measure. Did she make the right decision?

Explain how you arrived at your answer. Show all your work.

Stop

Name _____ Date _____

1 The thermometer below shows that the temperature is 3°C.

What would the temperature be if it were 5 degrees cooler?

A ⁻5°C
B ⁻2°C
C   2°C
D   8°C

2 Ramona recorded the daily temperature at noon for 5 days in a row. She recorded the following temperatures: 54°F, 66°F, 61°F, 59°F, and 63°F. What is the range of the temperatures?

A 66°F
B 54°F
C 22°F
D 12°F

Selected Response

Ask Yourself

Is the temperature positive or negative?

TEST TIPS

Selected Response

Ask Yourself

Do I add or subtract?

TEST TIPS

Go On

3   The table below shows the temperatures recorded in different Michigan cities.

City	Temperature
Ann Arbor	−15°F
Detroit	−18°F
Grand Rapids	−12°F
Sault Ste. Marie	−30°F

According to the table, which city has the highest temperature?

A Ann Arbor
B Detroit
C Grand Rapids
D Sault Ste. Marie

Ask Yourself

Where would each number fall on the thermometer?

TEST TIPS

4   The thermometer below shows the temperature when Keiko left for school one morning. While Keiko was in school, the temperature rose 12 degrees. When Keiko went to bed, the temperature had fallen 8 degrees. What was the temperature when Keiko went to bed?

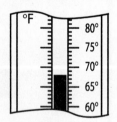

A 80°F
B 72°F
C 66°F
D 60°F

Ask Yourself

Should I count up or down?

TEST TIPS

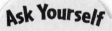
Go On

Name _____ Date _____

5 The Millers picked a total of 72 apples and pears from an orchard. They picked 18 more apples than pears. How many apples did they pick? How many pears did they pick?

Explain your thinking and show your work.

Constructed Response

Ask Yourself

What problem-solving strategy can I use to solve the problem?

TEST TIPS

Stop

Name _____ Date _____

1   Fran and her friends played a word game. The table below shows their final scores.

WORD GAME SCORES

Name	Score
Fran	35
Tom	28
Maria	20
Shana	20
Carlos	22

The range of scores increases by 10 if Karim's score is added to the table. Which of the following could be Karim's score?

A 45
B 35
C 25
D 20

2   The manager of the Thunderbolts baseball team recorded the number of home runs the team hit in each game. The table below shows the data. What is the median number of home runs the team hit in each game?

Game	Number of Home Runs Hit
1	2
2	4
3	1
4	2
5	0
6	2
7	3
8	1

A 1
B 2
C 3
D 4

Go On ▶

3 The table below shows the data collected in a survey of fourth graders.

WHAT IS YOUR FAVORITE AFTER SCHOOL ACTIVITY?

Activity	Number
Playing Basketball	7
Bicycling	15
Reading	8
In-line Skating	11
Playing Baseball	9

How many students altogether prefer in-line skating, bicycling, or playing basketball?

A 22
B 27
C 33
D 42

4 Mr. Bradley measured 6 of the dogs in the dog show. Then he listed their heights: 10 inches, 11 inches, 12 inches, 14 inches, 17 inches, 20 inches. What is the median height of the dogs?

A 10 inches
B 12 inches
C 13 inches
D 14 inches

Selected Response

Ask Yourself
What operation can I use to solve the problem?

TEST TIPS

Selected Response

Ask Yourself
How can I find the median when there are two middle numbers?

TEST TIPS

Go On

5   The data listed below shows the number of points scored by the Jaguars in 10 basketball games.

    42, 37, 52, 48, 45, 42, 40, 51, 39, 49

In the space below, make a table to organize the data. Don't forget to label your table.

Constructed Response

Ask Yourself
How many columns does the table need? How do I label each column?

TEST TIPS

What is the range of the basketball scores?

Explain how you found the answer.

Stop

1 Lauren makes a table to record her friends' heights.

Name	Height
Audra	125 centimeters
Keisha	130 centimeters
Mala	120 centimeters

Lauren wants to make a bar graph with the data in the table. Which of the following would be the most appropriate interval for the scale showing height in centimeters?

A 1

B 2

C 3

D 5

Selected Response

Ask Yourself

Does the scale need to show large or small numbers?

TEST TIPS

---

2 Use the graph shown below to answer the question.

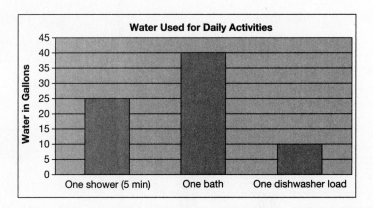

Peter, Paul, and Ron each take a shower. Peter also runs one dishwasher load. How many gallons of water do they use altogether?

A 85

B 80

C 75

D 60

Selected Response

Ask Yourself

What does the height of each bar represent?

TEST TIPS

Go On

3 The graph below shows the number of students in each grade at Westbrook School. What is the total number of students in Grades 3 and 4?

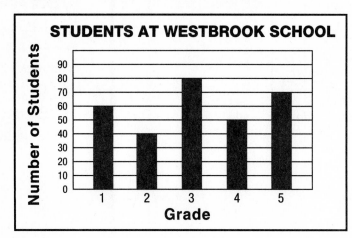

STUDENTS AT WESTBROOK SCHOOL

Number of Students / Grade

A 120
B 130
C 140
D 150

4 The graph below shows the number of miles Huong rode his bike each day last week. If Huong wants to ride 10 more miles this week than he did last week, how many miles should he ride this week?

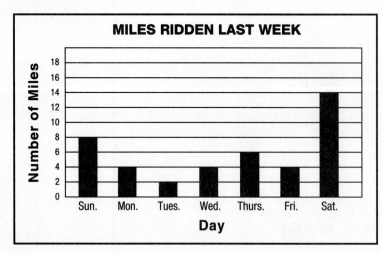

MILES RIDDEN LAST WEEK

Number of Miles / Day

A 34
B 44
C 54
D 64

Go On

Name _____ Date _____

5 Eric measured the water levels in 4 nearby ponds. The table below shows the data he recorded.

Water Levels in Ponds

Pond	Inches
Red Bird	16
Frog	10
Dragonfly	20
Mossy	14

Using the information in the table, make a bar graph below to show the water level in each pond.

Be sure to:

• title the graph

• include labels

• graph all the data

• use an appropriate scale

Ask Yourself

What should each bar show? What interval should I use on the scale?

TEST TIPS

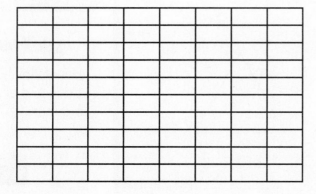

Look at your graph. How much higher is the water level in Mossy Pond than in Frog Pond?

Stop

1   Mariah draws the angle shown below on grid paper.

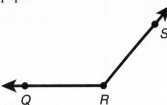

What kind of angle is ∠QRS?

A   acute
B   right
C   obtuse
D   straight

2   Which of the figures shown below is a regular pentagon?

A 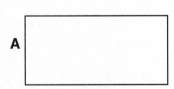   B

C 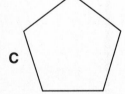   D

Go On

Name _____ Date _____

3 Which triangle has perpendicular sides?

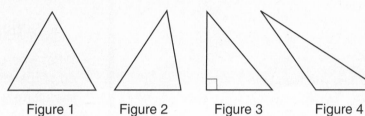

Figure 1   Figure 2   Figure 3   Figure 4

A Figure 1
B Figure 2
C Figure 3
D Figure 4

---

4 Classify the triangle shown below.

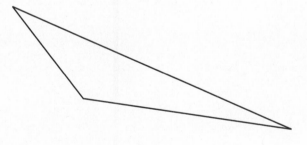

A equilateral
B isosceles
C scalene
D right

Go On

5 Joey said that all intersecting lines are perpendicular. Is he correct?

Use drawings to explain how you found the answer.

Constructed Response

Ask Yourself

What type of angles do perpendicular lines form?

TEST
TIPS

Stop

Name _____   Date _____

1   How many lines of symmetry does the figure
shown below have?

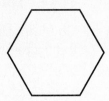

   A 7
   B 6
   C 5
   D 3

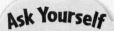

2   In which of the figures below is the dashed
line a line of symmetry?

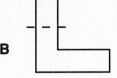

A   **B**

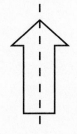

C   **D**

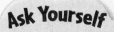

Go On ▶

Selected Response

3   Carla is making a border design around her room. She draws the figure shown below. The next figure in her design is a reflection of the figure over the line. What is the next figure in Carla's design?

Ask Yourself

Do I turn, flip, or slide the figure?

TEST
TIPS

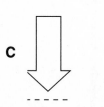

A

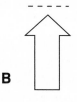

B

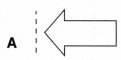

C

D

Selected Response

4   Which of the following figures has exactly 4 lines of symmetry?

A equilateral triangle
B square
C pentagon
D trapezoid

Ask Yourself

Do the two parts match?

TEST
TIPS

Go On

5   Damian's birthday is the 18th day of May. Since May is the 5th month, Damian wrote the date like this:

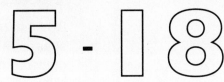

Constructed Response

Ask Yourself

Do the two parts match exactly after I draw a line of symmetry?

Damian says that all the numbers he wrote have line symmetry. Is he right?

Explain your thinking.

Choose one of the numbers Damian wrote. Using your ruler, draw a line of symmetry.

Using the same format as Damian, write a date for which all the numbers have line symmetry.

Stop

Name _____ Date _____

1   What is the difference between the area of the shaded portion and the area of the non-shaded portion for the figure below?

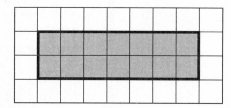

     A   8 units
     B   8 square units
     C   14 square units
     D   22 units

Selected Response

Ask Yourself

Do I use units or square units to measure the area of the figure?

TEST TIPS

2   The area of a square is 64 square inches. What is the length of one side of the square?

     A   6 inches
     B   8 inches
     C   12 inches
     D   32 inches

Selected Response

Ask Yourself

How can I use a formula to help me solve the problem?

TEST TIPS

Go On

3   Marie is pinning ribbon around the edges of a bulletin board. The board is 24 inches high and 36 inches wide. How many feet of ribbon does she need?

    A   5 feet
    B   10 feet
    C   60 feet
    D 120 feet

Selected Response

Ask Yourself

What formula can I use to find how many feet of ribbon Marie needs?

TEST TIPS

4   The perimeter of the figure below is 40 feet. What is the length of missing side x?

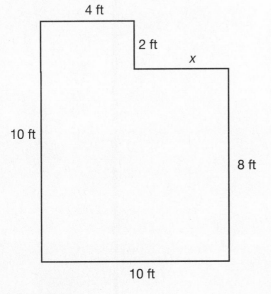

4 ft

2 ft

x

10 ft

8 ft

10 ft

    A   4 feet
    B   6 feet
    C   8 feet
    D 10 feet

Selected Response

Ask Yourself

How can I use the perimeter of the figure to find the missing length?

TEST TIPS

Go On

5   Michaela is planting a garden that is 16 feet long and 10 feet wide.

How many square feet of ground does the garden cover? Explain how you arrived at your answer. Show all your work.

Constructed Response

Ask Yourself

Can I draw a picture to solve the problem? Can I use formulas?

TEST
TIPS

Michaela also wants to build a fence around her garden. How many feet of fencing should she buy? Explain your thinking. Show all your work.

Stop

1   Rafael has these coins in his pocket.

What fraction of the coins in his pocket are pennies?

A $\dfrac{7}{3}$ **B** $\dfrac{7}{4}$

C $\dfrac{4}{7}$ **D** $\dfrac{3}{7}$

Selected Response

Ask Yourself

How many coins are there in all? How many coins are pennies?

TEST
TIPS

---

2   A gift shop sells boxes filled with mixed nuts. The table below shows the amount of each kind of nut in each gift box.

BOX OF NUTS

Kind of Nuts	Amount
Walnuts	$\frac{1}{2}$ cup
Pecans	$\frac{1}{4}$ cup
Cashews	$\frac{1}{8}$ cup

Which list shows the amounts of the different nuts ordered from **greatest** to **least**?

A $\dfrac{1}{2}$ cup, $\dfrac{1}{8}$ cup, $\dfrac{1}{4}$ cup   **B** $\dfrac{1}{4}$ cup, $\dfrac{1}{8}$ cup, $\dfrac{1}{2}$ cup

C $\dfrac{1}{2}$ cup, $\dfrac{1}{4}$ cup, $\dfrac{1}{8}$ cup   **D** $\dfrac{1}{8}$ cup, $\dfrac{1}{4}$ cup, $\dfrac{1}{2}$ cup

Selected Response

Ask Yourself

How can I compare fractions with unlike denominators?

TEST
TIPS

Go On

3 Jon's class takes a survey of students' favorite lunches. They find that $\frac{12}{16}$ of all the students prefer a chicken sandwich. Which of the fractions below are equivalent to $\frac{12}{16}$?

Selected Response

Ask Yourself

How do I know if fractions are equivalent?

TEST TIPS

A $\frac{3}{4}$ and $\frac{4}{8}$

B $\frac{6}{12}$ and $\frac{6}{8}$

C $\frac{3}{8}$ and $\frac{4}{12}$

D $\frac{3}{4}$ and $\frac{6}{8}$

4 Look at the figures shown below. Which improper fraction describes the shaded parts?

Selected Response

Ask Yourself

How many equal parts is each figure divided into?

TEST TIPS

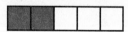

A $\frac{7}{5}$

B $\frac{12}{5}$

C $\frac{13}{5}$

D $\frac{16}{5}$

Go On

5   Meg is bringing cranberry, blueberry, and apple muffins to a bake sale. One-fourth of the muffins are cranberry, $\frac{3}{8}$ are blueberry, and 9 are apple. How many muffins does Meg bring?

Draw a picture to solve.

Explain how you found the answer. Show your work.

Ask Yourself

Can I draw a rectangle to model the problem?

TEST TIPS

Stop

1 Katie walks $\frac{1}{2}$ mile to Heidi's house. Then she walks $\frac{1}{4}$ mile to Randy's house. How far does Katie walk?

Ask Yourself

How do I add fractions with unlike denominators?

TEST TIPS

A $\frac{1}{6}$ mile

B $\frac{2}{6}$ mile

C $\frac{3}{4}$ mile

D $1\frac{2}{6}$ miles

---

2 Mrs. Tyler buys $1\frac{3}{4}$ pounds of potato salad and $1\frac{1}{4}$ pounds of macaroni salad. How much more potato salad than macaroni salad does she buy?

Ask Yourself

Is the answer in simplest form?

TEST TIPS

A $\frac{1}{4}$ pound

B $\frac{1}{2}$ pound

C $\frac{3}{4}$ pound

D $1\frac{1}{2}$ pounds

Go On

Name _____   Date _____

3 Mark wants to buy at least 1 pound of vegetables. The table below shows the vegetable packages sold in the grocery store. Which vegetable packages could Mark buy?

VEGETABLE PACKAGES

Package A	$\frac{7}{8}$ pound carrots
	$\frac{3}{4}$ pound celery
Package B	$\frac{1}{4}$ pound carrots
	$\frac{3}{8}$ pound peas
Package C	$\frac{5}{8}$ pound carrots
	$\frac{3}{4}$ pound turnips

A Packages A and B
B Packages B and C
C Packages A and C
D Packages A, B, and C

4 Van has a board that is $\frac{7}{8}$ yard long. He cuts $\frac{1}{4}$ yard off the board. How long is the piece of board he has left? Use the picture of fraction strips below to help you solve the problem.

| $\frac{1}{8}$ | $\frac{1}{8}$ | $\frac{1}{8}$ | $\frac{1}{8}$ | $\frac{1}{8}$ | $\frac{1}{8}$ | $\frac{1}{8}$ | $\frac{1}{8}$ |

| $\frac{1}{4}$ | ? |

A $\frac{6}{8}$ yard

B $\frac{5}{8}$ yard

C $\frac{4}{8}$ yard

D $\frac{3}{8}$ yard

Go On

5. Javier spends $\frac{1}{8}$ of his monthly allowance on baseball cards, $\frac{1}{4}$ on clothes, and $\frac{1}{4}$ on food. He saves the rest of his allowance so that he can buy a bike. What fraction of the allowance does Javier save each month?

Explain how you arrived at your answer. Show all your work.

Constructed Response

Ask Yourself

How many equal parts are there?

Javier's monthly allowance is $80. How many dollars does he spend on food, clothes, and baseball cards? How much money does Javier save each month?

Explain your thinking and show all your work.

Stop

Name _____ Date _____

1 Which decimal describes the model below?

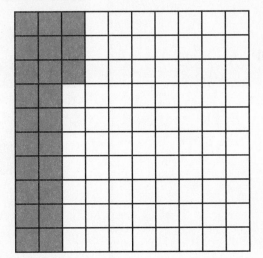

A 0.23
B 0.203
C 0.023
D 0.0023

Selected Response

Ask Yourself
How many squares are shaded? How many squares are there altogether?

TEST TIPS

2 At a gymnastics meet Matt earns the scores shown below.

9.65   8.6   9.45   8.99

Which list shows Matt's scores ordered from least to greatest?

A 8.6, 8.99, 9.45, 9.65
B 8.6, 9.45, 8.99, 9.65
C 9.65, 8.99, 9.45, 8.6
D 9.65, 9.45, 8.99, 8.6

Selected Response

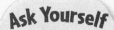
Ask Yourself
Where would each decimal be on a number line?

TEST TIPS

Go On

3 The Campbell family is on a canoe trip on Lake Michigan. The table below shows the numbers of miles they traveled each hour.

CAMPBELL FAMILY CANOE TRIP

Hour	Number of Miles Traveled
1	$1\frac{1}{5}$
2	1.35
3	1.67
4	$1\frac{4}{10}$
5	$1\frac{3}{4}$

During which hours did the Campbell family travel more than $1\frac{1}{2}$ miles?

A Hours 2 and 3   **B** Hours 2 and 5
C Hours 3 and 4   **D** Hours 3 and 5

---

4 Marcus lives 2.5 miles from school. Josh lives $2\frac{2}{5}$ miles from school. Barry lives $2\frac{1}{4}$ miles from school. Melissa lives 2.25 miles from school. Which two students live the same distance from school?

A Josh and Barry
B Barry and Melissa
C Melissa and Josh
D Josh and Melissa

Go On

5 Mr. Diaz is ordering caps for the players on his hockey team. The table shows the prices for caps.

CAP PRICES

Number of Caps	Price
1	$15.00
2	$26.50
3	$36.50
4	$45.00

If the pattern continues, what is the cost of 7 caps?

Explain how you found the answer. Show your work.

Constructed Response

Ask Yourself

Can I follow the pattern to solve the problem?

TEST TIPS

Stop

Name _____ Date _____

1 In January, an average of 28.7 cm of snow falls
   at O'Hare Airport in Illinois. In February, an
   average of 21.08 cm of snow falls at O'Hare.
   About how many more centimeters of snow
   fall at O'Hare in January than in February?

   A   6 cm
   B   8 cm
   C   18 cm
   D   50 cm

2 Adil's father totals the grocery bills from the
   past two weeks. The first bill is for $87.42.
   The second bill is for $94.36. How much
   money did he spend on groceries in the past
   two weeks?

   A   181.68
   B   181.78
   C   182.76
   D   182.70

Go On

3 Ahmad scored 748.08 points in the 10 meter diving competition. He beat Mathew by 17.52 points to win the gold medal. What was Mathew's score?

A 730.56
B 740.06
C 740.46
D 765.60

Selected Response

Ask Yourself

Should I add or subtract to solve the problem?

TEST
TIPS

4 The largest pumpkin at the State Agricultural Fair weighs 41.4 pounds. The second largest pumpkin weighs 32.2 pounds. What is the difference in weight between the two pumpkins?

A 8.2
B 9.2
C 9.6
D 10.2

Selected Response

Ask Yourself

Can I use addition to check my answer?

TEST
TIPS

Go On

Name _____   Date _____

5 Mike hiked four trails. The trails Mike hiked
and the trail lengths are shown below.

TRAILS MIKE HIKED

Trail	Length (in miles)
Bluff Ridge Trail	2.89
Basin Creek Trail	3.3
Cedar Ridge Trail	4.2
Craggy Gardens Trail	0.84

Ask Yourself

What operations should
I use? Did I align the
decimal points?

TEST
TIPS

What is the difference in miles between the
longest trail hiked and the shortest trail hiked?

Explain how you found the answer. Show
your work.

One day Mike hiked Basin Creek Trail in
the morning and Bluff Ridge Trail in the
afternoon. How many miles did he hike that
day altogether?
Explain your thinking. Show your work.

Stop

Date _____

1 Marina draws a right triangle on grid paper. Which of the following statements about Marina's triangle must be true?

A It has three right angles.
B It has one right angle.
C All of its sides are the same length.
D All of its angles are acute.

Selected Response

Ask Yourself

How can I describe a right angle?

TEST TIPS

2 Which of the following fractions is located between $\frac{1}{8}$ and $\frac{1}{2}$?

A $\frac{3}{4}$

B $\frac{2}{3}$

C $\frac{2}{8}$

D $\frac{1}{10}$

Selected Response

Ask Yourself

Where does each number lie on the number line?

TEST TIPS

Go On

Name _____   Date _____

3   The face of a cube has an area of 6 square
centimeters. What is the total area of all the
faces of the cube?

    A 60 square centimeters
    B 36 square centimeters
    C 24 square centimeters
    D 12 square centimeters

4   Which of the following does not have a
right angle?

    A regular pentagon
    B square
    C rectangle
    D right triangle

Go On

5   Mr. Lanuza wants to make a chart showing
the similarities and differences between a
triangular prism and a triangular pyramid.
Help Mr. Lanuza fill the chart.

Ask Yourself

Can I draw a diagram
to find the similarities
and differences?

TEST
TIPS

**Similarities between a Triangular Prism and a
Triangular Pyramid**

**Differences between a Triangular Prism and
a Triangular Pyramid**

Stop

1   How many edges does a square pyramid have?

    A 8
    B 6
    C 5
    D 4

Selected Response

Ask Yourself

Can I draw a picture to solve the problem?

TEST TIPS

---

2   An elevator climbs 5 floors in 10 seconds. How many minutes does it take to get to the 120th floor if it starts at the first floor?

    A 240 minutes
    B 120 minutes
    C   10 minutes
    D   4 minutes

Selected Response

Ask Yourself

How many seconds are there in a minute?

TEST TIPS

Go On

3 Marco spends $14.65 on dog food. He also buys a fish tank for $31.25. About how much more does Marco spend on the fish tank than on dog food?

  A $25
  B $20
  C $16
  D $8

Selected Response

Ask Yourself

Can I use rounding to estimate?

---

4 Latisha wants to place $\frac{11}{4}$ on a number line. Between which two numbers is $\frac{11}{4}$ located?

  A 1.5 and 2.0

  B $2\frac{1}{4}$ and $2\frac{2}{4}$

  C $\frac{1}{4}$ and $\frac{3}{4}$

  D $2\frac{1}{2}$ and 3

Selected Response

Ask Yourself

How do I compare fractions and decimals?

Go On

5. The 3 swimmers with the fastest times in the preliminary round qualify for the event final. The table below shows the results for the preliminary rounds of the women's 100 meters freestyle event.

Name	Time in Seconds
Maria A.	50.35
Sona M.	53.32
Jennifer S.	53.30
Shahla H.	58.61
Jody M.	50.13
Martina N.	52.26
Vivian L.	53.46
Jana N.	52.60
Leisha H.	56.04

Which three swimmers qualify for the event final? Explain how you got your answer.

How much faster is the winner of preliminary round than the swimmer in the last place?

Explain how you got your answer. Show all your work.

Constructed Response

Ask Yourself

Can I use additon to check my answer?

TEST TIPS

Name _____ Date _____

1 Which of the following figures has only one pair of parellel sides?

A square
B trapezoid
C rhombus
D parallelogram

Selected Response

Ask Yourself

How many sides does the figure have? How many are parallel?

TEST TIPS

---

2 Mr. Salazar's class made a rectangular banner 18 inches high. Its area is 1,296 square inches. How many feet long is the banner?

A   4 feet
B   6 feet
C   72 feet
D 108 feet

Selected Response

Ask Yourself

Can I use a formula to help me solve the problem?

TEST TIPS

Go On

3   Rob is trying to solve the following problem.

$$71.23 - 39.85 = \boxed{}$$

Which of the following is a reasonable estimate of the difference?

A 21
B 22
C 29
D 31

Ask Yourself

How can I tell if the estimate is reasonable?

---

4   At lunch, Alan drank $1\frac{3}{8}$ cups of water. At dinner, Alan drank $2\frac{6}{8}$ cups of water. How many cups of water did Alan drink at lunch and dinner in all?

A $3\frac{1}{8}$

B $3\frac{9}{16}$

C $4\frac{1}{8}$

D $4\frac{3}{8}$

Ask Yourself

What operation can I use to solve the problem?

Go On

5   Jeff has 3 boxes. There are 78 books in each
box. He takes all the books out of the boxes
and puts them onto 6 shelves. Each shelf has
the same number of books. How many books
are on each shelf?

Ask Yourself

Which operations
should I use to solve
the problem?

TEST
TIPS

Explain how you found the answer. Show
your work.

Jeff finds 2 more boxes of books. One box has
55 books and the other has 62 books. If he
continues to put the same number of books on
each shelf as before, how many shelves will
Jeff need altogether?
Explain your thinking and show all your work.

Stop

MEAP Practice Tests

1 Which of the following sets of numbers is ordered from **least** to **greatest**?

   A 358, 349, 340, 331
   B 340, 331, 358, 349
   C 331, 340, 358, 349
   D 331, 340, 349, 358

2 Marco has 129 pennies in his collection. Silvia has 138 pennies. What is the **best** estimate of how many pennies they have in all?

   A 170
   B 180
   C 270
   D 350

Go On

3 The school cafeteria can seat 186 students. Today, 91 fourth-graders and 78 fifth-graders are seated there. How many seats are still empty?

    A 27
    B 26
    C 19
    D 17

4 Ms. Castillo has 103 number cards. She gives an equal number of cards to each of the 4 study teams in her class. How many number cards does Ms. Castillo give to each team?

    A 26 with 1 left over
    B 25 with 3 left over
    C 24 with 3 left over
    D 23 with 2 left over

Go On

5   Ms. Flores conducted a survey of her students to find out how many books they read during the summer. The bar graph below shows the results of her survey.

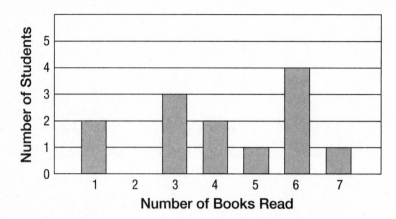

How many students read 4 books? Explain your thinking.

Sofia read more books than anyone else in the class. How many books did Sofia read? Explain how you got your answer. Show your work.

Name _____ Date _____

1 Which set of numbers can be written as a multiplication fact family?

    A 3, 7, 21
    B 3, 7, 25
    C 3, 5, 8
    D 3, 7, 10

2 Which is the **best** estimate for the weight of an apple?

    A 8 ounces
    B 6 pounds
    C 2 liters
    D 1 ounce

Go On

3 Midori plants 7 marigolds in her garden. She plants 5 times as many zinnias. How many more zinnias than marigolds does Midori plant?

A 35

B 33

C 28

D 24

4 The Allen family attends a Detroit Tigers baseball game. The clocks show the time they arrive at the stadium and the time they leave the stadium.

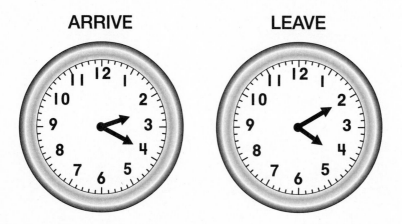

ARRIVE   LEAVE

How long are they at the stadium?

A 1 hour 20 minutes

B 1 hour 50 minutes

C 2 hours 50 minutes

D 4 hours 10 minutes

Go On

5   Marquita is packing books into bags for the used book sale.
She puts 8 books into each of the 7 bags.

How many books does Marquita pack? Explain how you got your answer and
show all your work.

Marquita adds 4 magazines to 2 of the bags and 3 magazines to 5 of the bags.
How many magazines does she pack?

Stop

1   Which of the following is another way to write $\frac{3}{5}$?

A $\frac{1}{2} + \frac{2}{3}$ **B** $\frac{2}{5} + \frac{1}{10}$

C $\frac{1}{5} + \frac{1}{4} + \frac{1}{3}$ **D** $\frac{1}{5} + \frac{1}{5} + \frac{1}{5}$

2   Which of the following is the most appropriate for measuring the area of your classroom?

A square inches
B square feet
C inches
D square miles

Go On

3   Which of these figures has parallel sides?

   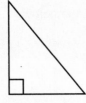   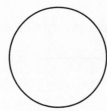   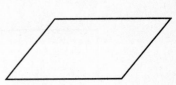

FIGURE 1   **FIGURE 2**   **FIGURE 3**   **FIGURE 4**

A Figure 1
B Figure 2
C Figure 3
D Figure 4

4   Which fraction stands for the part of the circle that is NOT shaded?

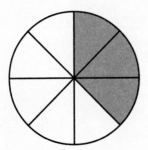

A $\frac{3}{4}$ **B** $\frac{5}{8}$

C $\frac{3}{8}$ **D** $\frac{1}{8}$

Go On

5   Mr. Chen is putting a fence around his flower garden. The garden is 22 feet long and 19 feet wide.

Label the length and width of each side on the figure below.

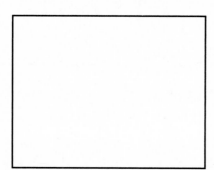

How much fencing does Mr. Chen need to buy?

Explain how you found the answer. Show your work.

1   When Europeans first arrived, about 15,000 Native Americans lived in the area that is now Michigan. What is another way to write 15,000?

   A   15 hundred
   B   1 thousand, 5 hundred
   C   15 thousand
   D   150 thousand

2   Jeremy is thinking of a number. The digit in the millions place is 6. The digit in the thousands place is 8 and the digit in the ones place is 4. Which of the following numbers could be Jeremy's number?

   A   608,154
   B   680,154
   C   6,908,504
   D   6,980,505

Go On ▶

3   The Mississippi River is about 2,300 miles long. How many hundreds of miles long is it?

A   2,300
B   230
C   23
D   2

4   Mr. Romero divides his class into 4 teams. He gives each team a problem to solve. The problem given to each team is shown below.

- Team 1: How many thousands are there in half a million?
- Team 2: How many hundreds are there in a hundred thousand?
- Team 3: How many hundreds are there in half a million?
- Team 4: How many tens make a hundred thousand?

If each team gets the correct answer, for which team is the answer 1,000?

A   Team 1
B   Team 2
C   Team 3
D   Team 4

Go On

5   Demetrius is playing a game. He picks four number cards. Use the clues below to find what cards he picks.

- Each card has a different number greater than 1 and less than 12.

- Three cards have odd numbers.

- The odd numbers are all less than the even number.

- The even number can be divided evenly by 4.

Explain how you found your answer. Show your work.

1 The table below shows the population of three different states.

State	Population
Alabama	4,447,100
Louisiana	4,468,976
South Carolina	4,012,012

Which of the following place values helps determine the state with the largest population?

A millions
B ten thousands
C hundred thousands
D thousands

2 Which number should be written in the box below to make the number sentence true?

$$267,841 > \boxed{}$$

A 268,041
B 267,998
C 267,899
D 267,481

Go On

3 What is the smallest even number that can be created using all the number cards shown below? Each digit can only be used once.

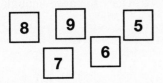

A 56,789
B 56,879
C 56.798
D 56,978

4 Sally, Jacob, Rosa, and Brent cleaned up a park on Saturday. The graph below shows about how many cans each person picked up. About how many more cans did Rosa pick up than Sally?

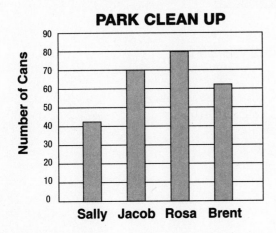

A about 40
B about 20
C about 10
D about 5

Go On

5 Tanya has 5 one-dollar bills and 5 quarters to buy lunch. She wants to order a grilled cheese sandwich, a garden salad, and lemonade.

Round each menu item Tanya wants to the nearest dollar. Does she have enough money to buy what she wants?

Lunch Menu

Chicken Sandwich	$4.65
Grilled Cheese	$2.85
Garden Salad	$1.75
Pasta Salad	$1.15
Bottled Water	$1.19
Lemonade	99¢

Explain how you found the answer. Show all your work.

1   Daniel went shopping at the store sale. He bought one pair of sneakers and 2 sunglasses. About how much money did he pay for those three items?

STORE SALE

Gloves	$8.46
Socks	$1.44 pair
Cap	$5.97
Sneakers	$20.99
Sunglasses	$7.82
Shirt	$14.79

A $17
B $27
C $37
D $47

2   The population of Riverside increased by 26,893 between 1990 and 2000. Which of the following sets of numbers represents the population of Riverside in 1990 and 2000?

A Population in 1990: 14,807; Population in 2000: 43,700
B Population in 1990: 16,000; Population in 2000: 43,000
C Population in 1990: 15,807; Population in 2000: 42,700
D Population in 1990: 23,012; Population in 2000: 48,985

Go On

3   Which of the following can be solved mentally using properties of addition?

    A 46 + 218 + 42
    B 191 + 421 + 9
    C 35 + 119 + 47
    D 17 + 239 + 48

4   In 2003 there were 25,283 runners entered in the Honolulu Marathon, and 22,161 of them finished the race. How many runners did NOT finish?

    A 3,231
    B 3,122
    C 3,022
    D   312

Go On

5   There are 761 books in Keisha's school's library. Dani's school has 685 books in its library.

How many more books does Keisha's school library have than Dani's? Explain how you found the answers. Show your work.

If Keisha's school's library gives 38 of its books to Dani's school's library, how many books will each library have then? Explain how you arrived at your answer. Show all your work.

Stop

1   Leah is training for the marathon. The table below shows her training goals for the first two weeks.

Week	Number of Training Sessions	Total Miles
Week 1	4	40
Week 2	5	60

At the beginning of each week Leah plans her training sessions so that she runs the same distance in each session that week. How many more miles does she run in a training session in the second week than a training session in the first week?

A   20 miles
B   12 miles
C   2 miles
D   1 mile

2   Campers at Camp Moosehead pose for a group photo. 48 campers sit on four benches and 16 campers stand behind the benches. If the four benches seat the same number of campers, how many campers does each bench seat?

A   6
B   8
C   12
D   16

Go On ▶

3   There are 8 students on a camping trip. There are 52 pretzels. Each student gets an equal number of pretzels. How many pretzels does each student get? How many pretzels are left over?

   A 6 with 4 left over
   B 6 with 6 left over
   C 7 with 2 left over
   D 8 with 4 left over

4   Amon plays a game of ring toss at the school fair and gets a score of 88. He tosses 4 rings into the outer circle, misses two tosses, and tosses the rest in the center circle.

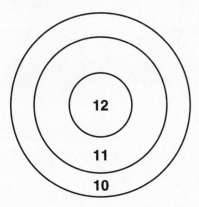

How many tosses did Amon try?

   A 4
   B 6
   C 10
   D 12

Go On

5   Andrew donates various items to a local hospital. The table below shows the items he want to donate, and the number of each item that he can pack in a box.

Items	Number of items per box
20 dishes	5
43 glasses	9
28 bowls	5
84 books	7

How many boxes will Andrew need?

Explain how you arrived at your answer. Show all your work.

Andrew can use his wagon to take 2 boxes at a time to his van. How many trips must he make to take all the boxes to the moving van?

Explain your answer.

Stop

1   Jason solves an equation. The solution to the equation is $y = 4$. Which of the following could be the equation Jason solves?

     A $y + 4 = 4$
     B $4y = 1$
     C $y + 8 = 4$
     D $y \div 2 = 2$

2   Toshi swims 6 times a week with the swim team. He swims 6,000 meters each week, swimming the same distance in each of the 6 training sessions. Which of the following shows the equation he used to find how many meters he swims in each session, and the correct solution to the equation?

     A $6x = 6{,}000$; 600 meters
     B $6x = 1{,}000$; 600 meters
     C $n = 6{,}000 \div 6$; 1,000 meters
     D $n \div 6 = 6{,}000$; 36,000 meters

Go On

3   The solutions to the equations below show Kasey and her sister Carla's ages. Their brother Manuel's age is the difference between Kasey and Carla's ages.

Kasey	$a \div 8 = 2$
Carla	$b \div 4 = 3$

How old is Manuel?

A 16
B 13
C 4
D 2

4   Laura, Rich, Robin, and April are playing a game. Each player gets to pick an equation and solve it. The player with the greatest solution advances on the game board.

Laura	Rich
$a \div 4 = 20$	$a \div 3 = 10$

Robin	April
$4a \div 4 = 20$	$a \div 6 = 15$

Assuming that all four players solve their equation to get the correct solution, who gets to advance on the game board?

A Laura
B Rich
C Robin
D April

Go On ▶

5 Jamie takes 56 photos of butterflies. She plans to put the photos on posters. Each poster holds 8 photos.

Let *p* stand for the number of posters. Write and solve an equation to find the number of posters Jamie needs.

Explain how you found your answer. Use words and symbols in your explanation.

Annalisa has half as many photos as Jamie. Her poster holds 4 photos each. How many posters does she need? Explain how you arrived at your answer. Show your work.

Stop

1   It takes 435 liters of water to grow enough wheat to make one loaf of bread. Estimate by rounding. About how many liters of water are needed to make 12 loaves of bread?

A 3,200 liters
B 3,600 liters
C 4,500 liters
D 6,500 liters

2   A concert will be held at Performance Theater. Each ticket costs $7. The theater's goal is to raise $12,000. If 1,893 people go to the concert, how much more money does the theater raise than its goal?

A $251
B $231
C $141
D $131

3   Kristi would like to earn money by walking her neighbors' dogs. She sees the following posters on a bulletin board.

Walk Trapper!

$3.25 each day
3 days a week

Walk Calvin!

$2.50 each day
4 days a week

How much money would Kristi earn each week if she takes both jobs?

A $19.75
B $19.50
C $18.75
D $5.75

4   The Cobra, a giant roller coaster, can carry 350 people at one time. Each hour the roller coaster makes 8 trips. If the roller coaster is filled during each trip, how many people can ride it in four hours?

A 12,200
B 11,200
C   2,800
D   1,400

Go On

5 During the summer, Mario and Alyssa won 24 ribbons in all for riding their horses at horse shows. Alyssa won twice as many ribbons as Mario. How many ribbons did they each win?

Explain how you found the answer. Show your work.

Rick won 10 more ribbons than Mario. Who won more ribbons, Rick or Alyssa?

Explain how you arrived at your answer. Show your work.

Stop

1   Lincoln High School buys 19 new filing cabinets for its library. If each filing cabinet costs \$485, about how much will the 19 filing cabinets cost?

     A   \$7,000
     B   \$10,000
     C   \$12,000
     D   \$16,000

2   There are 30 rooms on each floor of a 60-story building. If there are 4 lamps in each room, how many lamps are there in the building?

     A   72,000
     B   7,200
     C   1,800
     D   180

Go On

3   Kim earns $7.50 each hour working at a restaurant. She works 20 hours each week at the restaurant. Kim also earns $6.50 each hour working at a bookstore. She works 15 hours each week at the bookstore. How much does Kim earn altogether each week?

   A $337.50
   B $247.50
   C $231.50
   D $225.50

4   During the last two years, Mr. Tran drove 47 miles (round trip) each day to work. He worked 241 days in Year 1 and 237 days in Year 2. How many miles did Mr. Tran drive to work during the two years?

   A 23,646 miles
   B 22,566 miles
   C 22,466 miles
   D 21,466 miles

Go On

5   Rosa is on the school track team. She and her teammates want to buy 9 T-shirts for the team.

Summer Sale

T-shirts
$6.87

Rosa and her teammates decide to collect bottles for recycling. They get a nickel for every bottle they collect. About how many bottles do they need to collect to be able to buy the T-shirts?

Explain how you arrived at your answer. Show all your work.

Stop

1   Shawn has 9 times as many stamps now as he did 3 years ago. If Shawn has 810 stamps now, how many stamps did he have 3 years ago?

    A 900
    B 800
    C 90
    D 9

2   Manuel's cousins live in Lansing, Michigan. Manuel lives 440 miles away from them. It takes Manuel's mother 8 hours to drive to Lansing. How many miles does she drive each hour?

    A 65 miles
    B 55 miles
    C 6 miles
    D 5 miles

Go On

3   Tamika wants to buy a sled that costs $106. She has already saved $58. If she saves $4 each week, how many weeks will it take for her to save enough money to buy the sled?

   A 16
   B 15
   C 13
   D 12

4   Macy is cutting apples to bring to her running team's practice. She cuts each apple into 6 equal pieces. There are 24 girls on the running team. How many apples does Macy need to cut so that she will have 4 pieces for each girl?

   A 9
   B 14
   C 16
   D 22

Go On

5   Felipe makes cookies for sale. He makes a batch of 5,000 chocolate chip cookies. He packs ten cookies in each box. How many boxes does he need to pack all the chocolate chip cookies?

Explain how you got your answer. Show all your work.

Felipe also makes 84 sugar cookies. He layers the sugar cookies in a large cookie jar. If each layer has 6 cookies, how many layers are there in the jar? Explain how you arrived at your answer and show your work.

Use multiplication to check your answers. Show all your work.

Stop

1   Carlos, Jordan, and Kelsey have a jar with 252 marbles in it. They want to share
    the marbles equally. How many marbles will each receive?

    A 82
    B 84
    C 85
    D 87

2   Mr. Axford makes 208 burger patties for a barbeque. He wants to buy at least
    208 rolls to go with the burger patties. If the rolls come in packs of 6, 8, or 10,
    what is the fewest number of packs that he can buy?

    A 35
    B 26
    C 21
    D 20

Go On

3   Jane and Lee have 2,100 goats and 4,800 sheep on their farm. At night they lock the animals in three large pens. If each pen holds the same number of goats and sheep, how many animals does each pen have?

A 3,300
B 2,300
C 1,600
D   700

4   Shawn has 2,032 trading cards. He keeps the cards in 6 boxes with the same number of cards in each box. He keeps the leftover cards on his bookshelf. How many cards are on the bookshelf?

A 5
B 4
C 3
D 2

Go On

5   A store in Ann Arbor gets a shipment of 918 jeans and 216 T-shirts. The store manager arranges all the jeans on 9 shelves. He stacks the T-shirts on 6 shelves.

If each shelf holds the same number of jeans, how many jeans are on each shelf? Explain how you got your answer and show all your work.

Assuming that each of the 6 shelves holds the same number of T-shirts, how many T-shirts are there on each shelf? Explain how you arrived at your answer.

Show how you can use multiplication to check your answer.

Stop

1 LaShundra correctly listed all the factors of 36. Which of the following is LaShundra's list?

A 1, 2, 3, 5, 18, 24, 36

B 1, 2, 3, 4, 6, 12, 18, 36

C 1, 2, 3, 4, 6, 9, 12, 18, 36

D 1, 2, 3, 5, 6, 9, 12, 18, 24, 36

2 The picture below shows the shirts for some of the players on Eduardo's soccer team.

Which players have shirts with prime numbers on them?

A Eduardo and Rika

B Eduardo, Casey, and Alisa

C Shanna, Casey, and Alisa

D Eduardo, Alisa, and Rika

Go On

3 Yumiko wrote each factor of 30 on a different card. Then she draws 2 cards. Each card had a prime number. She did not draw an even number. What 2 cards did she draw?

A 3, 6
B 2, 3
C 3, 5
D 60, 90

4 Reggie is thinking of a number between 10 and 30. The number is a factor of 40 and a multiple of 4. What number is Reggie thinking of?

A 24
B 20
C 10
D 8

Go On

5   Rodney says that every multiple of 5 is also a multiple of 10. Is he right?
Explain your answer and show all your work.

Stop

1   The County Agricultural School raises chickens for sale. The school has 5,380
     chickens. The school keeps 880 chickens in a large henhouse and separates the
     rest of the chickens in 10 coops. If each of the coops holds the same number of
     chickens, how many chickens are there in each coop?

     A 880
     B 550
     C 480
     D 450

2   Mr. Suzuki has a collection of 1,980 stamps. He keeps them in 9 albums. Each
     album has the same number of stamps. Each album has 10 pages and each page
     holds the same number of stamps. How many stamps does each page have?

     A 22
     B 33
     C 220
     D 330

Go On

3   The game warden at a national park counts 3,720 pairs of adult seabirds. Each adult pair raises 3 chicks on average during the breeding season. About how many chicks will be raised at the national park during the season?

    A   11,100
    B   13,100
    C   111,000
    D   131,100

4   A group of volunteers works 5 days to build a playground. They work for 7 hours each day. They work a total of 945 hours. How many volunteers are there?

    A   27
    B   29
    C   270
    D   350

Go On

5   A family of 2 adults and 4 children visits the Children's Museum on Community Day. They pay a total of $26 for admission.

```
┌─────────────────────────────┐
│                             │
│       Community Day         │
│            at               │
│      Children's Museum      │
│                             │
│     SPECIAL ADMISSION       │
│                             │
│      Children: $2 each      │
│                             │
└─────────────────────────────┘
```

How much is an adult admission? Explain how you found the answer. Show your work.

On Community Day, how many children could accompany 3 adults for $40? Explain how you arrived at your answer and show all your work.

Stop

1   Jessica is 5 feet 2 inches tall. How many inches tall is she?

    A   68 inches
    B   62 inches
    C   58 inches
    D   56 inches

2   Which unit is appropriate for measuring how much the pencil shown below weighs?

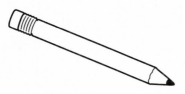

    A   degrees Celsius
    B   grams
    C   kilograms
    D   pounds

Go On

3   Caleb needs 40 ounces of cornmeal to bake muffins. The store only sells 1 lb, 2 lb, 4 lb, and 10 lb bags of corn meal. What is the smallest bag Caleb can buy so that he has enough corn meal for the muffins?

   A 1 lb bag
   B 2 lb bag
   C 4 lb bag
   D 10 lb bag

4   Use your ruler to help you solve this problem. Misti cut 100 pieces of ribbon the same size as shown below. How many meters of ribbon does she need altogether?

   A   3 meters
   B   5 meters
   C   8 meters
   D 12 meters

Go On

5   Yuki is cooking 4 cups of rice for a stew. The recipe recommends using half a gallon of chicken stock to cook the rice. Yuki uses 4 cups of chicken broth to cook the rice. Does she use enough chicken broth?

Explain how you arrived at your answer. Show all your work.

Yuki decides to make some more stew the next day. She buys 2 pints of chicken broth. If she uses the same recipe, how many cups of rice can she cook using the 2 pints of chicken broth?

Explain your thinking. Show all your work.

Stop

1   The thermometer below shows that the temperature is 3°C.

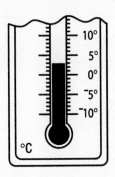

What would the temperature be if it were 8 degrees cooler?

A ⁻5°C
B ⁻3°C
C   3°C
D   5°C

2   Ricardo recorded the daily temperature at noon for 5 days in a row. He recorded the following temperatures:

65°F, 82°F, 73°F, 61°F, and 80°F.

What is the range of the temperatures?

A 82°F
B 61°F
C 21°F
D 19°F

Go On

3   The table below shows the temperatures recorded in different Michigan cities.

City	Temperature
Ann Arbor	⁻3°C
Detroit	⁻2°C
Grand Rapids	1°C
Sault Ste. Marie	⁻12°C

According to the table, which city has the lowest temperature?

A Detroit
B Grand Rapids
C Sault Ste. Marie
D Ann Arbor

4   The thermometer below shows the temperature when Elena left for school one morning. While Elena was in school, the temperature rose 12 degrees. When she went to bed, the temperature had fallen 8 degrees. What was the temperature when Elena went to bed?

A 83°F
B 72°F
C 70°F
D 58°F

Go On

5 The O'Neals picked a total of 61 oranges and tangerines from a citrus orchard. They picked 15 more oranges than tangerines. How many oranges did they pick? How many tangerines did they pick?

Explain your thinking and show your work.

Stop

1 Tracy and her friends played a word game. The table below shows their final scores.

WORD GAME SCORES

Name	Scores
Tracy	26
Corey	24
Jelena	28
Andrew	27
Mei Li	25

The range of scores increases by 5 if Anna's score is added to the table. Which of the following could be Anna's score?

A 32
B 29
C 19
D 18

2 The manager of the Hurricanes baseball team recorded the number of home runs the team hit in each game. The table at right shows the data.

What is the median number of home runs the team hit in each game?

A 1
B 2
C 3
D 4

Home Runs Hit by Hurricanes

Game	Number of Home Runs
1	2
2	3
3	1
4	4
5	0
6	3
7	4
8	5

Go On

3   The table below shows the data collected in a survey of fourth graders.

WHAT IS YOUR FAVORITE AFTER SCHOOL ACTIVITY?

Activity	Number
Playing Basketball	7
Bicycling	15
Reading	8
In-line Skating	11
Playing Baseball	9

How many students altogether prefer reading, bicycling, or playing baseball?

A 17
B 24
C 32
D 33

4   Ms. Peters weighed 6 of the dogs in the dog show. Then she listed their weights: 10 pounds, 13 pounds, 8 pounds, 16 pounds, 14 pounds, 11 pounds. What is the median weight of the dogs?

A 10 pounds
B 11 pounds
C 12 pounds
D 13 pounds

Go On

5 The data listed below shows the number of points scored by the Panthers in 10 basketball games.

43, 48, 36, 41, 45, 38, 54, 46, 40, 51

In the space below, make a table to organize the data. Don't forget to label your table.

What is the range of the basketball scores?

Explain how you found the answer.

Stop

1   Mia records the different types of books on her bookshelf in the table shown below.

Type of Book	Number of Books
Mystery	8
Biography	7
Science Fiction	9

She wants to make a bar graph with the data in the table. Which of the following would be the most appropriate interval for the scale showing the number of books?

A   10
B   5
C   4
D   1

2   Use the graph shown below to answer the question.

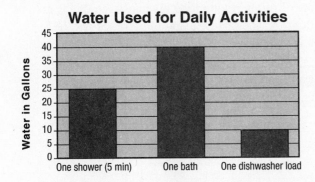

Water Used for Daily Activities

Ravi decides to take a shower instead of a bath. How much water will he save?

A   10
B   15
C   20
D   25

3 The graph below shows the number of students in each grade at Westbrook School. What is the total number of students in Grades 4 and 5?

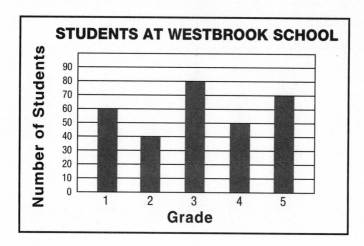

A 150
B 140
C 130
D 120

4 The graph below shows the number of miles Huong rode his bike each day last week. Huong wants to ride 50 miles this week. How many more miles will he have to ride this week than he did last week?

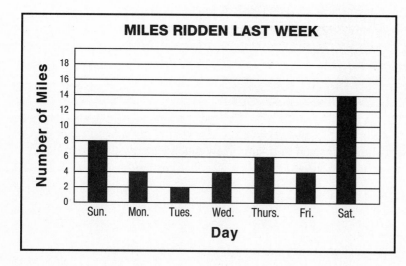

A 4
B 6
C 16
D 50

5   Jaime counted the kinds of wild flowers growing in 4 nearby parks. The table below shows the data he recorded.

Wild Flowers in Parks

Park	Number of Flowers
Armstrong	14
Zavala	6
Lakeview	20
Cityview	10

Using the information in the table, make a bar graph below to show the number of kinds of wild flowers in each park.

Be sure to:

• title the graph

• include labels

• graph all the data

• use an appropriate scale

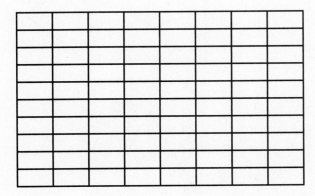

Look at your graph. How many more kinds of wild flowers grow in Lakeview Park than in Zavala Park?

1 Sherene draws the angle shown below on grid paper.

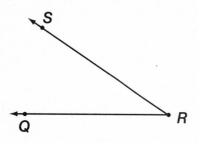

What kind of angle is ∠ *QRS*?

A right
B straight
C obtuse
D acute

2 Which of the figures shown below is a quadrilateral?

A
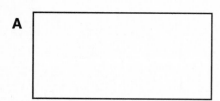

B

C
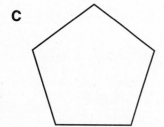

D
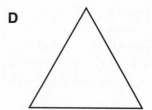

Go On

3   Which figure has perpendicular sides?

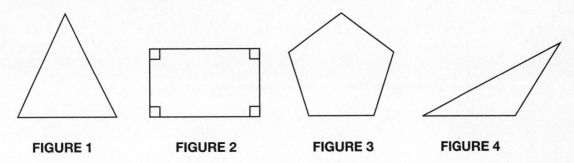

| FIGURE 1 | FIGURE 2 | FIGURE 3 | FIGURE 4 |

A Figure 1
B Figure 2
C Figure 3
D Figure 4

4   Classify the triangle shown below.

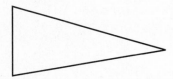

A right
B obtuse
C acute
D equilateral

Go On

5   Quincy said that all quadrilaterals have perpendicular sides. Is he correct?

Use drawings to explain how you found the answer.

Stop

Name _____ Date _____

1 How many lines of symmetry does the figure shown below have?

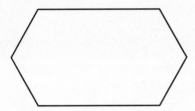

    A 5
    B 4
    C 3
    D 2

2 In which of the figures below is the dashed line a line of symmetry?

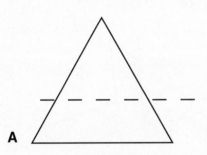

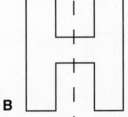

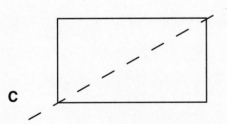

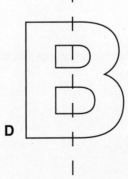

Go On

3   Kendra is making a border design around her room. She draws the figure shown below. The next figure in her design is a reflection of the figure over the line. What is the next figure in Kendra's design?

A

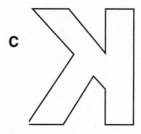

B

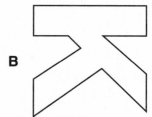

C

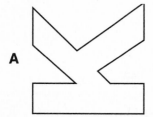

D

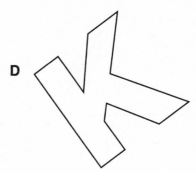

4   Which of the following figures has exactly 3 lines of symmetry?

A trapezoid
B circle
C square
D equilateral triangle

Go On

5   Omar Matthews wrote his initials like this:

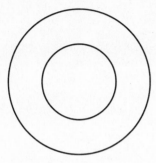

Omar says that both letters he wrote have line symmetry. Is he right?

Explain your thinking.

Choose one of the letters Omar wrote. Using your ruler, draw a line of symmetry.

Write your initials. Do the letters have a line of symmetry?
Explain your thinking.

Stop

1 What is the difference between the area of the shaded portion and the area of the non-shaded portion for the figure below?

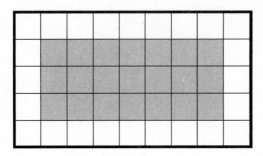

A 24 units
B 24 square units
C 3 units
D 3 square units

2 The area of a square is 81 square inches. What is the length of one side of the square?

A 18 inches
B 12 inches
C 9 inches
D 8 inches

Go On

3   Anita is taping ribbon around the edges of a poster. The poster is 16 inches long and 8 inches wide. How many feet of ribbon does she need?

A   3 feet
B   4 feet
C   12 feet
D   48 feet

4   The perimeter of the figure below is 52 feet. What is the length of missing side x?

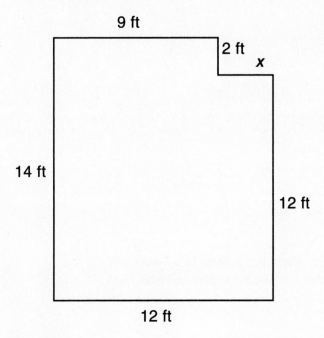

9 ft

2 ft

x

14 ft

12 ft

12 ft

A   6 feet
B   5 feet
C   4 feet
D   3 feet

Go On

5   Marisa is planting a garden that is 18 feet long and 9 feet wide.

How many square feet of ground does the garden cover?
Explain how you arrived at your answer. Show all your work.

Marisa also wants to build a fence around her garden. How many feet
of fencing should she buy? Explain your thinking. Show all your work.

Stop

1   Gilberto has these coins in his pocket.

What fraction of the coins in his pocket are dimes?

A $\frac{2}{5}$

B $\frac{4}{9}$

C $\frac{5}{9}$

D $\frac{9}{5}$

2   A gift shop sells boxes filled with mixed nuts. The table below shows the amount of each kind of nut in each gift box.

BOX OF NUTS

Kind of Nuts	Amount
Walnuts	$\frac{1}{6}$ cup
Pecans	$\frac{1}{2}$ cup
Cashews	$\frac{1}{3}$ cup

Which list shows the amounts of the different nuts ordered from **greatest** to **least**?

A $\frac{1}{6}$ cup, $\frac{1}{2}$ cup, $\frac{1}{3}$ cup

B $\frac{1}{6}$ cup, $\frac{1}{3}$ cup, $\frac{1}{2}$ cup

C $\frac{1}{2}$ cup, $\frac{1}{6}$ cup, $\frac{1}{3}$ cup

D $\frac{1}{2}$ cup, $\frac{1}{3}$ cup, $\frac{1}{6}$ cup

Go On

3   Jacob's class takes a survey of students' favorite lunches. They find that $\frac{16}{24}$ of all the students prefer pizza. Which of the fractions below are equivalent to $\frac{16}{24}$?

A $\frac{1}{2}$ and $\frac{2}{3}$ **B** $\frac{1}{2}$ and $\frac{4}{6}$

C $\frac{2}{3}$ and $\frac{4}{6}$ **D** $\frac{3}{4}$ and $\frac{2}{3}$

4   Look at the figures shown below. Which improper fraction describes the shaded parts?

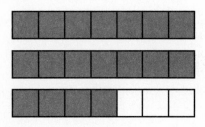

A $\frac{10}{7}$ **B** $\frac{11}{7}$

C $\frac{17}{7}$ **D** $\frac{18}{7}$

Go On

5   Molly is bringing cranberry, blueberry, and apple muffins to a bake sale.

One-third of the muffins are cranberry, $\frac{4}{9}$ are blueberry, and 10 are apple.

How many muffins does Molly bring?

Draw a picture to solve.

Explain how you found the answer. Show your work.

1   Brianna walks $\frac{1}{6}$ mile to Hannah's house. Then she walks $\frac{2}{3}$ mile to Armando's house. How far does Brianna walk?

    A $1\frac{5}{6}$ miles   **B** $\frac{5}{6}$ mile

    C $\frac{3}{6}$ mile   **D** $\frac{1}{3}$ mile

2   Mrs. Quinn buys $2\frac{5}{8}$ pounds of potato salad and $2\frac{3}{8}$ pounds of macaroni salad. How much more potato salad than macaroni salad does she buy?

    A $\frac{1}{8}$ pound   **B** $\frac{1}{4}$ pound

    C $\frac{3}{8}$ pound   **D** $1\frac{1}{8}$ pounds

3 Hakeem wants to buy less than 1 pound of vegetables. The table below shows the vegetable packages sold in the grocery store. Which vegetable package will Hakeem buy?

VEGETABLE PACKAGES

Package A	$\frac{7}{8}$ pound carrots $\frac{3}{4}$ pound celery
Package B	$\frac{1}{4}$ pound carrots $\frac{3}{8}$ pound peas
Package C	$\frac{5}{8}$ pound carrots $\frac{3}{4}$ pound turnips

A Package A
B Package B
C Package C
D Package B or Package C

4 Kelan has a board that is $\frac{9}{10}$ yard long. He cuts $\frac{2}{5}$ yard off the board. How long is the piece of board he has left?

Use the picture of fraction strips below to help you solve the problem.

$\frac{1}{10}$	$\frac{1}{10}$	$\frac{1}{10}$	$\frac{1}{10}$	$\frac{1}{10}$	$\frac{1}{10}$	$\frac{1}{10}$	$\frac{1}{10}$	$\frac{1}{10}$	$\frac{1}{10}$

$\frac{2}{5}$	?

A $\frac{4}{5}$ yard $\qquad$ **B** $\frac{3}{4}$ yard

C $\frac{3}{5}$ yard $\qquad$ **D** $\frac{1}{2}$ yard

Go On

5 Janet spends $\frac{1}{6}$ of her monthly allowance on books, $\frac{1}{6}$ on music, and $\frac{1}{3}$ on food. She saves the rest of her allowance so that she can buy a new computer.

What fraction of the allowance does Janet save each month?

Explain how you arrived at your answer. Show all your work.

Janet's monthly allowance is $90. How many dollars does she spend on books, music, and food? How much money does she save each month?

Explain your thinking and show all your work.

Stop

1   Which decimal describes the model below?

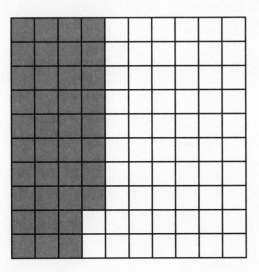

    A 0.0038
    B 0.038
    C 0.38
    D 3.80

2   At a gymnastics meet Derek earns the scores shown below.

2.7   3.8   3.6   2.9

Which list shows Derek's scores ordered from **least** to **greatest**?

    A 2.7, 2.9, 3.6, 3.8
    B 2.7, 3.6, 3.8, 2.9
    C 3.6, 2.7, 3.8, 2.9
    D 3.8, 3.6, 2.9, 2.7

Go On

3   The Campbell family is on a canoe trip on Lake Michigan. The table below shows the numbers of miles they traveled each hour.

CAMPBELL FAMILY CANOE TRIP

Hour	Number of Miles Traveled
1	$1\frac{1}{5}$
2	1.35
3	1.67
4	$1\frac{4}{10}$
5	$1\frac{3}{4}$

During which hour did the Campbell family travel less than $1\frac{1}{4}$ miles?

A Hour 1
B Hour 2
C Hour 3
D Hour 4

4   Dustin lives 1.25 miles from school. Jodi lives $1\frac{1}{2}$ miles from school. Luis lives $2\frac{1}{4}$ miles from school. Malia lives 1.5 miles from school. Which two students live the same distance from school?

A Jodi and Luis
B Dustin and Luis
C Malia and Dustin
D Jodi and Malia

Go On

5   Mr. Kee is ordering caps for the players on his hockey team. The table shows
     the prices for caps.

CAP PRICES

Number of Caps	Price
1	$16.00
2	$28.50
3	$39.00
4	$47.50

If the pattern continues, what is the cost of 6 caps?

Explain how you found the answer. Show your work.

Stop

1   In November, an average of 2.3 inches of rain falls in Orlando, Florida.
    In August, an average of 6.8 inches of rain falls in Orlando. To the
    nearest inch, about how many more inches of rain fall in Orlando in
    August than in February?

    A 2 inches
    B 5 inches
    C 6 inches
    D 8 inches

2   Shania's mother totals the grocery bills from the past two weeks. The first bill
    is for $73.81. The second bill is for $62.94. How much money did she spend on
    groceries in the past two weeks?

    A $135.75
    B $136.25
    C $136.75
    D $137.75

Go On

3   Kate scored 642.92 points in the 10 meter during competition. She beat Susan by 18.26 points to win the gold medal. What is Susan's score?

    A 661.44
    B 661.18
    C 624.66
    D 524.66

4   The largest watermelon at the State Agricultural Fair weights 34.6 pounds. The second largest watermelon weighs 26.8 pounds. What is the difference in weight between the two watermelons?

    A 61.4 pounds
    B 12.2 pounds
    C   8.2 pounds
    D   7.8 pounds

Go On

5   Mike hiked four trails. The trails Mike hiked and the trail lengths are shown below.

TRAILS MIKE HIKED

Trail	Length (in miles)
Bluff Ridge Trail	2.89
Basin Creek Trail	3.3
Cedar Ridge Trail	4.2
Craggy Gardens Trail	0.84

What is the difference in miles between the second longest trail hiked and Bluff Ridge Trail?

Explain how you found your answer. Show your work.

Mike hiked Craggy Gardens Trail on Friday and Cedar Ridge Trail on Saturday. How far did he hike altogether on Friday and Saturday?

Explain how you found the answer and show all your work.

Stop

1   Sherene draws a figure on grid paper. The figure has 4 sides and 4 right angles.
    All of its sides are the same length. What figure does she draw?

    A a right triangle
    B a pentagon
    C a trapezoid
    D a square

2   Which of the following fractions is located between $\frac{1}{9}$ and $\frac{1}{3}$?

    A $\frac{2}{9}$ **B** $\frac{1}{2}$

    C $\frac{2}{3}$ **D** $\frac{4}{9}$

Go On

3 The face of a cube has an area of 16 square centimeters. What is the total area of all the faces of the cube?

    A   64 square centimeters
    B   80 square centimeters
    C   96 square centimeters
    D 160 square centimeters

4 Which of the following figures has at least one right angle?

    A equilateral triangle
    B regular pentagon
    C rectangle
    D regular hexagon

Name _____ Date _____

5 Ms. Tomas wants to make a chart showing the similarities and differences between a cube and a square pyramid. Help Ms. Tomas fill the chart.

Similarities between a Cube and a Square Pyramid

Differences between a Cube and a Square Pyramid

Name _____ Date _____

1   How many vertices does a triangular pyramid have?

    A 1
    B 2
    C 3
    D 4

2   An elevator climbs 5 floors in 10 seconds. How many minutes does it take to get to the 90th floor if it starts at the first floor?

    A 2 minutes
    B 3 minutes
    C 180 minutes
    D 450 minutes

3 Marcia spends $13.20 on a CD. She also spends $33.82 on books. About how much more does Marcia spend on the books than she does on the CD?

A $11

B $21

C $30

D $31

4 Ling wants to place $\frac{9}{4}$ on a number line. Between which two numbers is $\frac{9}{4}$ located?

A $1\frac{1}{4}$ and $1\frac{3}{4}$

B 1.9 and 2.0

C 2.0 and 2.5

D 1.0 and 1.5

Go On

5 The 3 swimmers with the fastest times in the preliminary round qualify for the event final. The table below shows the results for the preliminary rounds of the men's 100 meters freestyle event.

Name	Time in Seconds
Chris H.	46.23
Russell D.	49.25
Ali R.	48.46
Timothy F.	49.22
Malcolm R.	46.78
Romero A.	50.37
Liang T.	48.04
Jan T.	51.34
Koji M.	48.64

Which three swimmers qualify for the event final?
Explain how you got your answer.

How much faster is the winner of preliminary round than the swimmer in the last place?
Explain how you got your answer. Show all your work.

Stop

Name ______________________ Date ____________

1 Which of the following figures has only one pair of perpendicular sides?

A rectangle
B rhombus
C right triangle
D equilateral triangle

2 Ms. Owen's class made a rectangular banner 24 inches high. Its area is 2,016 square inches. How many feet long is the banner?

A 168 feet
B 84 feet
C 6 feet
D 5 feet

Go On

3   Rita is trying to solve the following problem.

$$64.08 - 47.29 = \boxed{}$$

Which of these is a reasonable estimate of the difference?

A   17
B   23
C   30
D   100

4   At lunch, Jay drank $1\frac{3}{4}$ cups of milk. At dinner, Jay drank $2\frac{2}{4}$ cups of milk.

How many cups of milk did he drink at lunch and dinner in all?

A $3\frac{1}{4}$ **B** $4\frac{1}{4}$

C $4\frac{2}{4}$ **D** $4\frac{3}{4}$

Go On

5 Bryan has 4 boxes. There are 86 baseball cards in each box. He takes all the baseball cards out of the boxes and puts them onto 8 shelves. Each shelf has the same number of baseball cards. How many baseball cards are on each shelf?

Explain how you found the answer. Show your work.

Bryan finds 3 more boxes of baseball cards. These boxes have 72, 68, and 75 baseball cards in them. If Bryan continues to put the same number of baseball cards on each shelf as he did earlier, how many shelves will Brian need altogether?

Explain your thinking. Show your work.

Stop

MEAP Teacher Guide

Answer Key and Correlations

Item	Answer	GLE
MEAP Guided Practice 1		
1	B	N.ME.03.02
2	C	N.FL.03.07
3	A	N.MR.03.15
4	D	N.ME.03.21
5	see p. 178	D.RE.03.01
MEAP Guided Practice 2		
1	C	N.MR.03.09
2	C	M.UN.03.01
3	B	N.MR.03.15
4	C	M.PS.03.12
5	see p. 178	N.MR.03.15
MEAP Guided Practice 3		
1	B	N.ME.03.19
2	C	M.UN.03.03
3	B	G.GS.03.02
4	B	N.ME.03.16
5	see p. 179	M.PS.03.13
MEAP Guided Practice 4		
1	D	N.ME.04.02
2	D	N.ME.04.02
3	B	N.ME.04.03
4	B	N.ME.04.03
5	see p. 179	N.MR.04.37
MEAP Guided Practice 5		
1	A	N.ME.04.03
2	D	N.ME.04.01
3	A	N.ME.04.01
4	B	D.RE.04.03
5	see p. 180	N.FL.04.34
MEAP Guided Practice 6		
1	B	N.FL.04.36
2	C	N.FL.04.08
3	D	N.FL.04.08
4	A	N.MR.04.37
5	see p. 180	N.MR.04.37
MEAP Guided Practice 7		
1	D	D.RE.04.03
2	B	N.FL.04.14
3	B	N.FL.04.14
4	B	N.MR.04.37
5	see p. 181	D.RE.04.03

Item	Answer	GLE
MEAP Guided Practice 8		
1	B	N.FL.04.12
2	A	N.FL.04.12
3	A	N.FL.04.12
4	B	N.FL.04.12
5	see p. 181	N.FL.04.12
MEAP Guided Practice 9		
1	C	N.FL.04.34
2	D	N.FL.04.14
3	B	N.MR.04.37
4	C	N.FL.04.14
5	see p. 182	N.MR.04.37
MEAP Guided Practice 10		
1	C	N.FL.04.34
2	C	N.FL.04.14
3	D	N.MR.04.37
4	B	N.MR.04.37
5	see p. 182	N.FL.04.37
MEAP Guided Practice 11		
1	B	N.FL.04.37
2	C	N.FL.04.14
3	A	N.MR.04.37
4	B	N.MR.04.37
5	see p. 183	N.FL.04.14
MEAP Guided Practice 12		
1	C	N.FL.04.14
2	C	N.FL.04.14
3	B	N.FL.04.37
4	C	N.FL.04.14
5	see p. 183	N.MR.04.37
MEAP Guided Practice 13		
1	C	N.ME.04.04
2	B	N.MR.04.06
3	B	D.AN.05.03
4	C	N.ME.04.04
5	see p. 184	N.ME.04.04
MEAP Guided Practice 14		
1	C	N.FL.04.14
2	B	N.FL.04.14
3	A	N.FL.04.34
4	B	N.MR.04.37
5	see p. 184	N.MR.04.37

Answer Key and Correlations

Item	Answer	GLE
MEAP Guided Practice 15		
1	C	M.TE.04.05
2	C	M.UN.04.01
3	B	M.TE.04.05
4	B	M.UN.04.01
5	see p. 185	N.MR.04.35
MEAP Guided Practice 16		
1	B	M.UN.04.03
2	D	D.RE.04.02
3	C	M.UN.04.03
4	B	M.UN.04.03
5	see p. 185	N.MR.04.37
MEAP Guided Practice 17		
1	A	D.RE.04.02
2	B	D.RE.04.02
3	C	D.RE.04.03
4	C	D.RE.04.02
5	see p. 186	D.RE.04.01
MEAP Guided Practice 18		
1	A	D.RE.04.01
2	A	D.RE.04.03
3	B	D.RE.04.03
4	C	D.RE.04.03
5	see p. 186	D.RE.04.01
MEAP Guided Practice 19		
1	C	M.TE.04.10
2	C	G.GS.04.02
3	C	G.GS.04.01
4	C	G.GS.04.02
5	see p. 187	G.GS.04.01
MEAP Guided Practice 20		
1	B	G.TR.04.04
2	D	G.TR.04.04
3	A	G.TR.04.05
4	B	G.TR.04.04
5	see p. 188	G.TR.04.04
MEAP Guided Practice 21		
1	B	M.TE.04.06
2	B	M.TE.04.08
3	B	M.TE.04.06
4	B	M.MR.04.24
5	see p. 188	M.TE.04.06

Answer Key and Correlations

Item	Answer	GLE
MEAP Guided Practice 22		
1	D	N.ME.04.20
2	C	N.MR.04.26
3	D	N.MR.04.21
4	B	N.MR.04.25
5	see p. 189	N.MR.04.37
MEAP Guided Practice 23		
1	C	N.MR.04.37
2	B	N.MR.04.37
3	C	N.MR.04.37
4	B	N.FL.04.28
5	see p. 189	N.MR.04.37
MEAP Guided Practice 24		
1	A	N.ME.04.15
2	A	N.ME.04.18
3	D	N.MR.04.37
4	B	N.MR.04.37
5	see p. 190	N.MR.04.37
MEAP Guided Practice 25		
1	B	N.MR.04.37
2	B	N.FL.04.32
3	C	N.FL.04.32
4	B	N.FL.04.32
5	see p. 190	N.MR.04.37
MEAP Guided Practice 26		
1	B	G.GS.04.02
2	C	N.MR.04.23
3	B	M.PS.04.09
4	A	G.GS.04.02
5	see p. 191	G.SR.04.03
MEAP Guided Practice 27		
1	A	G.SR.04.03
2	D	M.TE.04.05
3	C	M.FL.04.34
4	D	N.MR.04.22
5	see p. 192	N.FL.04.32
MEAP Guided Practice 28		
1	B	G.GS.04.01
2	B	M.PS.04.11
3	D	N.FL.04.34
4	C	N.MR.04.37
5	see p. 192	N.MR.04.37

SCORING RUBRICS
Guided Practice

Guided Practice 1, Item 5

A **4-point** response includes all of the following:
- Indicates correct answers for both questions in the item.
  - o 8 students read fewer than 6 books.
  - o The range of the data is 6.
- Provides a clear explanation of how each answer was derived. For example: I looked at all the bars to the left of the bar above the number 6, then I added: $2 + 0 + 3 + 2 + 1 = 8$. To find the range, I subtracted the fewest number of books read from the most books read. $7 - 1 = 6$, so the range is 6.

A **3-point** response includes the following:
- Correct answers for both questions in the item
- Explanation that shows good understanding of the questions and how to find the answers, but
- Explanation is missing a step or is otherwise unclear.

A **2-point** response includes the following:
- Correct answer to one question, but not both
- Answer to other question is incorrect, unclear, or missing.
- Explanation shows some understanding of bar graphs and finding the range of data, but lacks clarity.

A **1-point** response includes the following:
- A partial response on one of the questions; attempts to answer are unclear or only partially correct.
- Explanation exhibits limited understanding of bar graphs.
- Does not explain how to find the range of data.

A **0-point** response shows little or no understanding of the problem. No attempt is made to explain the work and all answers are incorrect.

Guided Practice 2, Item 5

A **4-point** response includes all of the following:
- Indicates correct answers for both questions in the item.
  - o Chaz needs 42 granola bars.
  - o Chaz uses 22 stickers.
- Provides a clear explanation of how each answer was derived. For example: Chaz wants 7 bars in each of 6 bags. $6 \times 7 = 42$. Chaz uses 22 stickers. $3 \times 4 = 12$; $5 \times 2 = 10$; $12 + 10 = 22$.

A **3-point** response includes the following:
- Correct answers for both questions in the item
- Explanation that shows good understanding of the questions and how to find the answers, but
- Explanation is missing some steps or is otherwise unclear.

A **2-point** response includes the following:
- Correct answer to one question, but not both
- Answer to other question is incorrect, unclear, or missing.
- Explanation shows some understanding of division and multiplication, but lacks clarity.

A **1-point** response includes the following:
- A partial response on one of the questions; attempts to answer are unclear or only partially correct.
- Explanation exhibits limited understanding of division and/or multiplication.

A **0-point** response shows little or no understanding of the problem. No attempt is made to explain the work and all answers are incorrect.

Guided Practice 3, Item 5

A **4-point** response includes all of the following:
- Indicates correct answers for both questions in the item.
  - o Long sides should be labeled 20 feet; short sides should be labeled 15 feet.
  - o 70 feet
- Provides a clear explanation of how the answer was derived. For example: First, I labeled the length and width of the room. Then I added the lengths of the 4 sides together to find the perimeter of the room. The total is the number of feet of wallpaper border Mr. Willis needs to buy for the living room: 70 feet.

A **3-point** response includes the following:
- Correct answers for both questions in the item
- Explanation that shows good understanding of the questions and how to find the answers, but
- Explanation is missing some labels or is otherwise unclear.

A **2-point** response includes the following:
- Correct answer to one question, but not both
- Answer to other question is incorrect, unclear, or missing.
- Explanation shows some understanding of perimeter but lacks clarity.

A **1-point** response includes the following:
- A partial response on one of the questions; attempts to answer are unclear or only partially correct.
- Explanation exhibits limited understanding of perimeter.
- Does not explain how to find the perimeter.

A **0-point** response shows little or no understanding of the problem. No attempt is made to explain the work and all answers are incorrect.

Guided Practice 4, Item 5

A **4-point** response includes all of the following:
- Indicates correct answer for the question in the item.
  - o Juan picked cards with the numbers 2, 4, 6, and 7.
- Provides a clear explanation of how the answer was derived. For example: 2, 4, and 6 are less than 7. 2, 4, and 8 are less than 9. 4, 6, and 8 are less than 9. 9 can be divided evenly by 1, 3, and 9, so I know the odd number is not 9. 7 can be divided evenly only by 1 and 7. So the numbers are 2, 4, 6, and 7.
- Demonstrates the ability to identify a number that can be divided evenly only by itself and 1.
- All work is clearly shown

A **3-point** response includes the following:
- Correct answer for the question in the item
- Explanation that shows good understanding of the question and how to find the answer, but
- Explanation is missing some steps or is otherwise unclear.

A **2-point** response includes the following:
- Answer to question is only partially correct or unclear.
- Explanation shows some understanding of odd, even, and prime numbers but lacks clarity.

A **1-point** response includes the following:
- Attempts to answer are unclear or only partially correct.
- Explanation exhibits limited understanding of odd, even, and prime numbers.

A **0-point** response shows little or no understanding of the problem. No attempt is made to explain the work and all answers are incorrect.

Guided Practice 5, Item 5

A **4-point** response includes all of the following:

- Indicates correct answer for the question in the item.
  - o Yes, Beth has enough money.
- Provides a clear explanation of how the answer was derived. For example: When I round to the near-est dollar, $2.85 rounds to $3, $1.15 rounds to $1, and 99¢ rounds to $1. $3 + $1 + $1 = $5. Beth has $6 altogether because 5 one-dollar bills and 4 quarters are equal to $6. Since $5 < $6, Beth has enough money.
- Demonstrates the ability to count money.
- Demonstrates the ability to round to the nearest dollar.

A **3-point** response includes the following:

- Correct answer for the question in the item
- Explanation that shows good understanding of the question and how to find the answer, but
- Explanation is missing some steps or is otherwise unclear.

A **2-point** response includes the following:

- Answer to question is only partially correct or unclear.
- Explanation shows some understanding of rounding but lacks clarity.
- Explanation shows some understanding of counting money but lacks clarity.

A **1-point** response includes the following:

- Attempts to answer are unclear or only partially correct.
- Explanation exhibits limited understanding of rounding and counting money.

A **0-point** response shows little or no understanding of the problem. No attempt is made to explain the work and the answer is incorrect.

Guided Practice 6, Item 5

A **4-point** response includes all of the following:

- Indicates correct answers for both questions in the item.
  - o There are 178 more students in Hopkins Elementary than in West Ridge Elementary.
  - o 819 students in Hopkins Elementary; 747 students in West Ridge Elementary
- Provides a clear explanation of how each answer was derived. For example: I found the difference by subtracting the smaller number from the larger number. 872 − 694 = 178. To find the number of students in each school after 53 students moved, I subtracted 53 from 872 to find the number of stu-dents in Hopkins Elementary. 872 − 53 = 819. I added 53 to 694 to find the number of students in West Ridge Elementary. 694 + 53 = 747.

A **3-point** response includes the following:

- Correct answers for both questions in the item
- Explanation that shows good understanding of the questions and how to find the answers, but
- Explanation is missing a step or is otherwise unclear.

A **2-point** response includes the following:

- Correct answer to one of the questions, but not both
- Answer to other question is incorrect, unclear, or missing.
- Explanation shows some understanding of addition and subtraction, but lacks clarity.

A **1-point** response includes the following:

- A partial response on one of the questions; attempts to answer are unclear or only partially correct.
- Explanation exhibits limited understanding of addition and subtraction.

A **0-point** response shows little or no understanding of the problem. No attempt is made to explain the work and all answers are incorrect.

Guided Practice 7, Item 5

A **4-point** response includes all of the following:
- Indicates correct answers for both questions in the item.
  - o 28 boxes
  - o 14 trips
- Provides a clear explanation of how each answer was derived. For example: I divided 27 by 5. The answer is 5 with a remainder of 2. Kortney will need 5 boxes, plus another one for the remaining 2 dishes. Then I divided for the rest of the items. $40 \div 7 = 5$ R5 (6 boxes needed), $20 \div 5 = 4$, $72 \div 6 = 12$. Then I added $6 + 6 + 4 + 12 = 28$. Kortney needs 28 boxes. To find the number of trips, I divided the number of boxes (28) by the number of boxes per trip (2). $28 \div 2 = 14$.

A **3-point** response includes the following:
- Correct answers for both questions in the item
- Explanation that shows good understanding of the question and how to find the answer, but
- Explanation is missing a step or is otherwise unclear.

A **2-point** response includes the following:
- Correct answer to one of the questions, but not both
- Answer to other question is incorrect, unclear, or missing.
- Explanation shows some understanding of division, but lacks clarity.

A **1-point** response includes the following:
- A partial response on one of the questions; attempts to answer are unclear or only partially correct.
- Explanation exhibits limited understanding of division.

A **0-point** response shows little or no understanding of the problem. No attempt is made to explain the work and all answers are incorrect.

Guided Practice 8, Item 5

A **4-point** response includes all of the following:
- Indicates correct answers for both questions in the item.
  - o $4p = 36$; $p = 9$; 9 album pages; Possible explanation: 36 = total number of photos. p = number of album pages Carrie needs. Each album page holds 4 photos, so $4p = 36$; $4p \div 4 = 36 \div 4$; $p = 9$. Carrie needs 9 album pages.
  - o Brooke has 3 times as many photos as Carrie, so I multiplied to find how many photos Brooke has. $36 \times 3 = 108$. Each of Brooke's album pages holds 6 photos; so $6p = 108$; $6p \div 6 = 108 \div 6$; $p = 18$. Brooke needs 18 album pages.
- Uses both words and symbols in the explanation.

A **3-point** response includes the following:
- Correct answers for both questions in the item
- Explanation that shows good understanding of the questions and how to find the answers, but
- Explanation is missing some steps or is otherwise unclear.

A **2-point** response includes the following:
- Correct answer to one of the questions, but not both
- Answer to other question is incorrect, unclear, or missing.
- Explanation shows some understanding of writing and solving an equation, but lacks clarity.

A **1-point** response includes the following:
- A partial response on one of the questions; attempts to answer are unclear or only partially correct.
- Explanation exhibits limited understanding of writing and solving an equation.

A **0-point** response shows little or no understanding of the problem. No attempt is made to explain the work and all answers are incorrect.

Guided Practice 9, Item 5

A **4-point** response includes all of the following:
- Indicates correct answer for both parts of the question in the item.
  - o Sara won 18 ribbons. Michael won 9 ribbons.
  - o Sara
- Provides a clear explanation of how the answer was derived. For example: I used Guess-and-Check to find the correct numbers. I looked for numbers that had a sum of 27 with one number twice as great as the other. First guess: Sara wins 20 ribbons. Michael wins 7 ribbons. $20 + 7 = 27$; $2 \times 7 \neq 20$. Second guess: Sara wins 19 ribbons. Michael wins 8 ribbons. $19 + 8 = 27$; $2 \times 8 \neq 19$. Third guess: Sara wins 18 ribbons. Michael wins 9 ribbons. $18 + 9 = 27$; $2 \times 9 = 18$. This guess was correct. Roberto won 8 more ribbons than Michael. $9 + 8 = 17$. Roberto won 17 ribbons. Since $18 > 17$, Sara won more ribbons than Roberto.
- Demonstrates the ability to add and multiply to find the correct answer

A **3-point** response includes the following:
- Correct answer for both questions in the item
- Explanation that shows good understanding of the questions and how to find the answers, but
- Explanation is missing some steps or is otherwise unclear.

A **2-point** response includes the following:
- Correct answer to one of the questions, but not both
- Answer to other question is incorrect, unclear, or missing.
- Explanation shows some understanding of addition and multiplication but lacks clarity.

A **1-point** response includes the following:
- Attempts to answer are unclear or only partially correct.
- Explanation exhibits limited understanding of addition and multiplication.

A **0-point** response shows little or no understanding of the problem. No attempt is made to explain the work and the answer is incorrect.

Guided Practice 10, Item 5

A **4-point** response includes all of the following:
- Indicates correct answer for the question in the item.
  - o They need to collect about 1,100 cans.
- Provides a clear explanation of how the answer was derived. For example: First I multiplied to find the cost of 8 T-shirts. $8 \times \$6.87 = \$54.96$. They collect a nickel for every can, so they need 20 cans to get a dollar. I rounded $54.96 to $55. Then I mulitplied to estimate the number of cans. $20 \times 55 = 1,100$. Ryan and his teammates need about 1,100 cans to get enough money to buy 8 T-shirts.
- Work is clearly shown.

A **3-point** response includes the following:
- Correct answer for the question in the item
- Explanation that shows good understanding of the question and how to find the answer, but
- Explanation is missing some steps or is otherwise unclear.

A **2-point** response includes the following:
- Answer to question is only partially correct or unclear.
- Explanation shows some understanding of estimation and multiplication.
- Does not explain estimation clearly.

A **1-point** response includes the following:
- Attempts to answer are unclear or only partially correct.
- Explanation exhibits limited understanding of multiplication, and estimation.
- Does not explain how to use estimation to find out if the answer is reasonable.

A **0-point** response shows little or no understanding of the problem. No attempt is made to explain the work and the answer is incorrect.

Guided Practice 11, Item 5

A **4-point** response includes all of the following:
- Indicates correct answer for the question in the item.
  - o 9 necklaces
  - o 440 bracelets
- Provides a clear explanation of how the answer was derived. For example: I divided to find how many groups of 8 are in 72. 72 ÷ 8 = 9. 72 silver beads will make 9 necklaces. To find how many bracelets I divided 4,400 by 10 and got 440. 4,400 glass beads will make 440 bracelets. To check my answers: $9 \times 8 = 72$ and $440 \times 10 = 4,400$.

A **3-point** response includes the following:
- Correct answer for the questions in the item
- Explanation that shows good understanding of the questions and how to find the answers, but
- Explanation is missing some steps or is otherwise unclear.

A **2-point** response includes the following:
- Answers to questions are only partially correct or unclear.
- Explanation shows some understanding of division but lacks clarity.

A **1-point** response includes the following:
- Attempts to answer are unclear or only partially correct.
- Explanation exhibits limited understanding of division.

A **0-point** response shows little or no understanding of the problem. No attempt is made to explain the work and the answer is incorrect.

Guided Practice 12, Item 5

A **4-point** response includes all of the following:
- Indicates correct answer for the questions in the item.
  - o 106 jeans
  - o 24 shirts
- Provides a clear explanation of how the answer was derived. For example: 848 ÷ 8 = 106 so 106 jeans are on each shelf. 144 ÷ 6 = 24 so there are 24 shirts on each shelf. I check the answers using multiplication. $106 \times 8 = 848$. $24 \times 6 = 144$.

A **3-point** response includes the following:
- Correct answer for the questions in the item
- Explanation that shows good understanding of the questions and how to find the answers, but
- Explanation is missing some steps or is otherwise unclear.

A **2-point** response includes the following:
- Answers to questions are only partially correct or unclear.
- Explanation shows some understanding of problem solving but lacks clarity.

A **1-point** response includes the following:
- Attempts to answer are unclear or only partially correct.
- Explanation exhibits limited understanding of divison and problem solving.

A **0-point** response shows little or no understanding of the problem. No attempt is made to explain the work and the answer is incorrect.

Guided Practice 13, Item 5

A **4-point** response includes all of the following:
- Indicates correct answer for the question in the item.
  - o   Yes. A number that has 10 as a factor will also have 5 as a factor.
- Provides a clear explanation of how the answer was derived. For example: The factors of 10 are 1, 2, 5, and 10. Since 5 is a factor of 10 then any number that has 10 as a factor will also have 5.
- Demonstrates an understanding of factors.

A **3-point** response includes the following:
- Correct answer for the question in the item
- Explanation that shows good understanding of the question and how to find the answer, but
- Explanation is missing some steps or is otherwise unclear.

A **2-point** response includes the following:
- Answer to question is only partially correct or unclear.
- Explanation shows some understanding of factors but lacks clarity.

A **1-point** response includes the following:
- Explanation exhibits limited understanding of factors.

A **0-point** response shows little or no understanding of the problem. No attempt is made to explain the work and the answer is incorrect.

Guided Practice 14, Item 5

A **4-point** response includes all of the following:
- Indicates correct answer for the questions in the item.
  - o   Adult admission is $7.00.
  - o   4 children
- Provides a clear explanation of how the answers were derived. For example: I multiplied to find the cost of admission for the children. $3 \times \$2 = \$6$. Then I subtracted the children's admission from the total admission to find the admission for 2 adults. $\$20 - \$6 = \$14$. I divided by 2 to find the admission for 1 adult. $\$14 \div 2 = \$7$. To find how many children could go with 4 adults for $36, I first multiplied 4 by $7 and got $28. $\$36 - \$28 = \$8$. $\$8 \div \$2 = 4$ so 4 children could go.
- Demonstrates an understanding of multiplication and division.

A **3-point** response includes the following:
- Correct answers for the questions in the item
- Explanation that shows good understanding of the questions and how to find the answers, but
- Explanation is missing some steps or is otherwise unclear.

A **2-point** response includes the following:
- Answers to questions are only partially correct or unclear.
- Explanation shows some understanding of problem solving, multiplication, and division but lacks clarity.

A **1-point** response includes the following:
- Attempts to answer are unclear or only partially correct.
- Explanation exhibits limited understanding of problem solving, multiplication, and division.

A **0-point** response shows little or no understanding of the problem. No attempt is made to explain the work and the answer is incorrect.

Guided Practice 15, Item 5

A **4-point** response includes all of the following:
- Indicates correct answers for both questions in the item.
  - o No, Laney did not make the right decision.
- Provides a clear explanation of how each answer was derived. For example: When you round 1.35 meters to the nearest meter you get 1 meter. If Laney bought a piece of glass 1 meter high it would be too short to fix the window. She made the wrong decision. Sometimes with measurements you shouldn't estimate.
- All work is clearly shown

A **3-point** response includes the following:
- Correct answers for the question in the item
- Explanation that shows good understanding of the question and how to find the answer, but
- Explanation is missing a step or is otherwise unclear.

A **2-point** response includes the following:
- Answer to question is only partially correct or unclear.
- Explanation shows some understanding of measurement and estimation but lacks clarity.

A **1-point** response includes the following:
- A partial response on one part of the question; attempts to answer are unclear or only partially correct.
- Explanation exhibits limited understanding of measurement and estimation.

A **0-point** response shows little or no understanding of the problem. No attempt is made to explain the work and the answer is incorrect.

Guided Practice 16, Item 5

A **4-point** response includes all of the following:
- Indicates correct answer for both questions in the item.
  - o 45 apples
  - o 27 pears
- Provides a clear explanation of how the answer was derived. For example: I used the Guess-and-Check strategy to find the answer. First I guessed 40 apples and 32 pears, for a total of 72. That would make only 8 more apples than pears, which is not enough apples. Then I guessed 48 apples and 24 pears. That would make 24 more apples than pears, which is too many apples. Finally I tried 45 apples and 27 pears. This works because 45 + 27 = 72, and there are 18 more apples than pears.
- Demonstrates the ability to use a problem solving strategy to find the correct answer.

A **3-point** response includes the following:
- Correct answer for both questions in the item
- Explanation that shows good understanding of the question and how to find the answer, but
- Explanation is missing some steps or is otherwise unclear.

A **2-point** response includes the following:
- Correct answer to only one of the questions, but not both
- Answer to the other question is incorrect, unclear, or missing.
- Explanation shows some understanding of problem solving but lacks clarity.

A **1-point** response includes the following:
- Attempts to answer are unclear or only partially correct.
- Explanation exhibits limited understanding of problem solving.

A **0-point** response shows little or no understanding of the problem. No attempt is made to explain the work and the answer is incorrect.

Guided Practice 17, Item 5

A **4-point** response includes all of the following:
- Indicates correct answer for both parts of the question in the item.
  - o

Game	Points Scored
1	42
2	37
3	52
4	48
5	45
6	42
7	40
8	51
9	39
10	49

  - o The range of the basketball scores is 15.
- Provides a clear explanation of how the range was derived. For example: I subtracted the least score in the table from the greatest score. $52 - 37 = 15$. The range of the basketball scores is 15.
- The table is labeled accurately.

A **3-point** response includes the following:
- Correct answer for both parts of the question in the item
- Explanation that shows good understanding of the question and how to find the answer, but
- Table is missing some labels or is otherwise unclear.

A **2-point** response includes the following:
- Correct answer to only one part of the question
- Answer to the other part is incorrect, unclear, or missing.
- Explanation shows some understanding of how to find the range of data but lacks clarity.

A **1-point** response includes the following:
- Attempts to answer are unclear or only partially correct.
- Explanation exhibits limited understanding of finding the range of data.

A **0-point** response shows little or no understanding of the problem. No attempt is made to explain the work and the answer is incorrect.

Guided Practice 18, Item 5

A **4-point** response includes all of the following:
- Indicates correct answer for both parts of the question in the item.
  - o

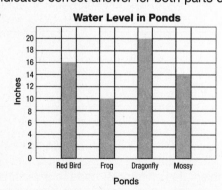

  - o The water level is 4 inches higher in Mossy Pond than in Frog Pond.
- The graph is titled, includes labels, and has an appropriate scale.
- All the data is graphed accurately.

A **3-point** response includes the following:
- Correct answer for both parts of the question in the item
- Explanation that shows good understanding of the question and how to find the answer, but
- Graph is missing some labels or is otherwise unclear.

A **2-point** response includes the following:
- Correct answer to only one part of the question
- Answer to the other part is incorrect, unclear, or missing.
- Explanation shows some understanding of bar graphs but lacks clarity.

A **1-point** response includes the following:
- Attempts to answer are unclear or only partially correct.
- Explanation exhibits limited understanding of bar graphs.

A **0-point** response shows little or no understanding of the problem. No attempt is made to explain the work and the answer is incorrect.

Guided Practice 19, Item 5

A **4-point** response includes all of the following:
- Indicates correct answer for the question in the item.
  - o No, Joey is not correct.
- Provides a clear explanation of how the answer was derived. For example: Joey is incorrect because intersecting lines may or may not be perpendicular.
- Includes drawings to demonstrate intersecting lines that are perpendicular and not perpendicular.

A **3-point** response includes the following:
- Correct answer for the question in the item
- Explanation that shows good understanding of the question and how to find the answer, but
- Explanation is missing some drawings or is otherwise unclear.

A **2-point** response includes the following:
- Answer to question is only partially correct or unclear.
- Explanation shows some understanding of perpendicular lines but lacks clarity.

A **1-point** response includes the following:
- Attempts to answer are unclear or only partially correct.
- Explanation exhibits limited understanding of perpendicular lines.

A **0-point** response shows little or no understanding of the problem. No attempt is made to explain the work and the answer is incorrect.

Guided Practice 20, Item 5

A **4-point** response includes all of the following:
- Indicates correct answers for each part of the question in the item.
  - o no
  - o The number 1 or the number 8 with a line of symmetry drawn through the number.
    Possible answers:

  - o *Possible answers:* 8—11, 1—18
- Provides a clear explanation of how the answer to the first part of question was derived. For example: Damian is incorrect because if the number 5 were cut out, there is no way to fold it in half so that the two parts would match exactly.

A **3-point** response includes the following:
- Correct answers for all three parts of the question
- Explanation that shows good understanding of the question and how to find the answer, but
- Explanation is unclear.

A **2-point** response includes the following:
- Correct answer to only one part of the question
- Answer to other parts is incorrect, unclear, or missing.
- Explanation shows some understanding of line symmetry but lacks clarity.

A **1-point** response includes the following:
- A partial response on one part of the question; attempts to answer are unclear or only partially correct.
- Explanation exhibits limited understanding of line symmetry.

A **0-point** response shows little or no understanding of the problem. No attempt is made to explain the work and all answers are incorrect.

Guided Practice 21, Item 5

A **4-point** response includes all of the following:
- Indicates correct answers for both questions in the item.
  - o 160 square feet
  - o 52 feet of fencing
- Provides a clear explanation of how each answer was derived. For example: To find how many square feet of ground the garden covers, I needed to find the area. I used the formula for the area of a rectangle: $A = l \times w$; $A = 16$ feet $\times 10$ feet; $A = 160$ square feet. To find how much fencing is needed to go around the garden, I needed to find the perimeter. I used the formula for the perimeter of a rectangle: $P = (2 \times l) + (2 \times w)$. $P = (2 \times 16$ feet$) + (2 \times 10$ feet$)$; $P = 32$ feet $+ 20$ feet; $P = 52$ feet

A **3-point** response includes the following:
- Correct answers for both questions in the item
- Explanation that shows good understanding of the questions and how to find the answers, but
- Explanation is unclear.

A **2-point** response includes the following:
- Correct answer to one question, but not both
- Answer to other question is incorrect, unclear, or missing.
- Explanation shows some understanding of area and perimeter but lacks clarity.

A **1-point** response includes the following:
- A partial response on one of the questions; attempts to answer are unclear or only partially correct.
- Explanation exhibits limited understanding of area and perimeter.

A **0-point** response shows little or no understanding of the problem. No attempt is made to explain the work and all answers are incorrect.

Guided Practice 22, Item 5

A **4-point** response includes all of the following:
- Indicates correct answer for the question in the item.
  - o Meg brings 24 muffins.
- Provides a clear explanation of how the answer was derived. For example: I drew a rectangle to represent all the muffins. Then I separated it into 8 equal parts. I know that $\frac{1}{4} = \frac{2}{8}$, so $\frac{2}{8}$ of the muffins are cranberry. $\frac{3}{8}$ of the muffins are blueberry. 9 apple muffins are $\frac{3}{8}$ of all the muffins. So each $\frac{1}{8}$ equals 3 muffins. $8 \times 3 = 24$. Meg brings 24 muffins.
- Includes a drawing to illustrate the solution.

A **3-point** response includes the following:
- Correct answer for the question in the item
- Explanation that shows good understanding of the question and how to find the answer, but
- The drawing is missing or is unclear.

A **2-point** response includes the following:
- Answer to question is only partially correct or unclear.
- Explanation shows some understanding of a problem solving strategy and fraction concept but lacks clarity.

A **1-point** response includes the following:
- Attempts to answer are unclear or only partially correct.
- Explanation exhibits limited understanding of problem solving and fractions.

A **0-point** response shows little or no understanding of the problem. No attempt is made to explain the work and the answer is incorrect.

Guided Practice 23, Item 5

A **4-point** response includes all of the following:
- Indicates correct answers for the questions in the item.
  - o Javier saves $\frac{3}{8}$ of his monthly allowance.
  - o Javier spends $20 on food, $20 on clothes, and $10 on baseball cards. He saves $30 each month.
- Provides a clear explanation of how the answers were derived. For example: I added the fractions that Javier spends on food, clothes, and baseball cards. $\frac{1}{4} + \frac{1}{4} + \frac{1}{8} = \frac{5}{8}$. Then I subtracted $\frac{5}{8}$ from the total to find the fraction that he saves. $1 - \frac{5}{8} = \frac{3}{8}$.

  I found the fractional parts of the monthly allowance to find the amounts Javier spends on diffrent things. $\frac{1}{4}$ of $80 = $20. So, Javier spends $20 on clothes and $20 on food. $\frac{1}{8}$ of $80= $10. So, Javier spends $10 on baseball cards. $\frac{3}{8}$ of $80 = $30. Javier saves $30 each month.

- All work is clearly shown

A **3-point** response includes the following:
- Correct answer for both questions in the item
- Explanation that shows good understanding of the questions and how to find the answer, but
- Shown work is missing or is unclear.

A **2-point** response includes the following:
- Correct answer to only one question in the item.
- Explanation shows some understanding of fractions, but lacks clarity.

A **1-point** response includes the following:
- Attempts to answer are unclear or only partially correct.
- Explanation exhibits limited understanding of fractions.

A **0-point** response shows little or no understanding of the problem. No attempt is made to explain the work and the answer is incorrect.

Guided Practice 24, Item 5

A **4-point** response includes all of the following:
- Indicates correct answer for the question in the item.
  - o Seven caps will cost $61.50.
- Provides a clear explanation of how the answer was derived. For example: First I looked for a pattern in the table. The pattern is to add $11.50 to the first amount and $1.50 less to each amount after that. I continued the pattern to find the answer. 4 caps cost $45.00. $45.00 + $7.00 = $52.00, so 5 caps cost $52.00. $52.00 + $5.50 = $57.50, so 6 caps cost $57.50. $57.50 + $4.00 = $61.50, so 7 caps cost $61.50.
- All work is clearly shown.

A **3-point** response includes the following:
- Correct answer for the question in the item
- Explanation that shows good understanding of the question and how to find the answer, but
- Shown work is missing or is unclear.

A **2-point** response includes the following:
- Answer to question is only partially correct or unclear.
- Explanation shows some understanding of a problem solving strategy but lacks clarity.

A **1-point** response includes the following:
- Attempts to answer are unclear or only partially correct.
- Explanation exhibits limited understanding of problem solving.

A **0-point** response shows little or no understanding of the problem. No attempt is made to explain the work and the answer is incorrect.

Guided Practice 25, Item 5

4-point response includes all of the following:
- Indicates correct answer for the questions in the item.
  - o 3.36 miles
  - o 6.19 miles
- Provides a clear explanation of how the answer was derived. For example: First I looked in the table to find the length of the longest trail. The Cedar Ridge Trail is 4.2 miles long. Then I looked in the table to find the length of the shortest trail. The Craggy Gardens Trail is 0.84 mile long. Finally, I subtracted to find the difference: 4.2 − 0.84 = 3.36.
  First I looked in the table to find the length of each trail Mike hiked. Basin Creek Trail is 3.3 miles long, and Bluff Ridge Trail is 2.89 miles long. Then I added to find the total distance Mike hiked. 3.3 + 2.89 = 6.19. Mike hiked 6.19 miles altogether.

A **3-point** response includes the following:
- Correct answer for both questions in the item
- Explanation that shows good understanding of the questions and how to find the answers, but
- Explanation is missing some steps or is otherwise unclear.

A **2-point** response includes the following:
- Answer to the questions are only partially correct or unclear.
- Explanation shows some understanding of interpreting tables and decimal operations, but lacks clarity.

A **1-point** response includes the following:
- Attempts to answer are unclear or only partially correct.
- Explanation exhibits limited understanding of interpreting tables and operations decimals.

A **0-point** response shows little or no understanding of the problem. No attempt is made to explain the work and the answer is incorrect.

Guided Practice 26, Item 5

A **4-point** response includes all of the following:
- Indicates correct answers for both parts of the question.
  - o Similarities: Both have at least one triangular face. Both are 3-dimensional. All faces are flat (no curved faces).
  - o Differences: Different number of faces, edges, and vertices.

A **3-point** response includes the following:
- Correct answers for both parts of the question
- Explanation that shows good understanding of the question and how to find the answer, but
- Explanation is missing a step or is otherwise unclear.

A **2-point** response includes the following:
- Correct answer to only one part
- Answer to other part is incorrect, unclear, or missing.
- Explanation shows some understanding of 3-dimensional solids, but lacks clarity.

A **1-point** response includes the following:
- A partial response on one part of the question; attempts to answer are unclear or only partially correct.
- Explanation exhibits limited understanding of 3-dimensional solids.

A **0-point** response shows little or no understanding of the problem. No attempt is made to explain the work and all answers are incorrect.

Guided Practice 27, Item 5

A **4-point** response includes all of the following:
- Indicates correct answers for both questions in the item.
  - o   Jody M., Maria A., and Martina N. qualify for the event final.
  - o   8.48 seconds
- Provides a clear explanation of how the answers were derived. For example: I ordered all the times in the table to find the three fastest times. The three swimmers with the lowest times were Jody M., Maria A., and Martina N.

  I ordered all the times in the table to find the fastest swimmer (Jody M.—50.13). Shahla H. had the slowest time—58.61. I subtracted to find the difference. 58.61 – 50.13. Jody M. was 8.48 seconds faster than Shahla H.

A **3-point** response includes the following:
- Correct answers for both questions in the item
- Explanation that shows good understanding of the questions and how to find the answers, but
- Explanation is missing a step or is otherwise unclear.

A **2-point** response includes the following:
- Correct answer to only one of the questions in the item
- Answer to other question is incorrect, unclear, or missing.
- Explanation shows some understanding of decimal place value and operations, but lacks clarity.

A **1-point** response includes the following:
- A partial response on one of the questions; attempts to answer are unclear or only partially correct.
- Explanation exhibits limited understanding of decimal place value and operations.

A **0-point** response shows little or no understanding of the problem. No attempt is made to explain the work and all answers are incorrect.

Guided Practice 28, Item 5

A **4-point** response includes all of the following:
- Indicates correct answer for both questions in the item.
  - o   There are 39 books on each shelf.
  - o   Jeff needs 9 shelves altogether.
- Provides a clear explanation of how the answers were derived. For example: First I multiplied the number of boxes, 3, by the number of books in each box, 78, to find the total number of books $3 \times 78 = 234$. There are a total of 234 books. Then I divided the total number of books, 234, by the number of shelves, 6, to find the number of books on each shelf. $234 \div 6 = 39$. There are 39 books on each shelf.

  I added to find out how many more books Jeff found. $55 + 62 = 117$. Before, Jeff had 234 books, so I added to find how many books Jeff had altogether. $117 + 234 = 351$. Now Jeff has 351 books. He puts 39 books on each shelf, so I divided to see how many shelves he needs. $351 \div 39 = 9$. Jeff needs 9 shelves altogether.
- All work is clearly shown.

A **3-point** response includes the following:
- Correct answer for both questions in the item
- Explanation that shows good understanding of the questions and how to find the answers, but
- Explanation is missing some steps or is otherwise unclear.

A **2-point** response includes the following:
- Answer to questions are only partially correct or unclear.
- Explanation shows some understanding of using multiplication and division, but lacks clarity.

A **1-point** response includes the following:
- Attempts to answer are unclear or only partially correct.
- Explanation exhibits limited understanding of using multiplication and division.

A **0-point** response shows little or no understanding of the problem. No attempt is made to explain the work and the answer is incorrect.

Item	Answer	GLE
MEAP Practice Test 1		
1	D	N.ME.03.03
2	C	N.FL.03.07
3	D	N.MR.03.15
4	B	N.MR.03.14
5	see p. 198	D.RE.03.01
MEAP Practice Test 2		
1	A	N.MR.03.09
2	A	M.UN.03.01
3	C	N.MR.03.15
4	B	M.PS.03.12
5	see p. 198	N.MR.03.15
MEAP Practice Test 3		
1	D	N.ME.03.19
2	B	M.UN.03.03
3	D	G.GS.03.02
4	B	N.ME.03.16
5	see p. 199	M.PS.03.13
MEAP Practice Test 4		
1	C	N.ME.04.02
2	C	N.ME.04.02
3	C	N.ME.04.03
4	C	N.ME.04.13
5	see p. 199	N.MR.04.37
MEAP Practice Test 5		
1	B	N.MR.04.37
2	D	N.ME.04.01
3	C	N.ME.04.01
4	A	D.RE.04.03
5	see p. 200	N.FL.04.34
MEAP Practice Test 6		
1	C	N.FL.04.36
2	B	N.FL.04.08
3	B	N.FL.04.08
4	B	N.MR.04.37
5	see p. 200	N.MR.04.37
MEAP Practice Test 7		
1	C	D.RE.04.03
2	C	N.FL.04.14
3	A	N.FL.04.14
4	B	N.MR.04.37
5	see p. 201	D.RE.04.03

Item	Answer	GLE
MEAP Practice Test 8		
1	D	N.FL.04.12
2	C	N.FL.04.12
3	C	N.FL.04.12
4	D	N.FL.04.12
5	see p. 201	N.FL.04.12
MEAP Practice Test 9		
1	B	N.FL.04.34
2	A	N.FL.04.14
3	A	N.MR.04.37
4	B	N.FL.04.14
5	see p. 202	N.MR.04.37
MEAP Practice Test 10		
1	B	N.FL.04.34
2	B	N.FL.04.14
3	B	N.MR.04.37
4	C	N.MR.04.37
5	see p. 202	N.FL.04.37
MEAP Practice Test 11		
1	C	N.FL.04.37
2	B	N.FL.04.14
3	D	N.MR.04.37
4	C	N.MR.04.37
5	see p. 203	N.FL.04.14
MEAP Practice Test 12		
1	B	N.FL.04.14
2	C	N.FL.04.14
3	B	N.FL.04.37
4	B	N.FL.04.14
5	see p. 203	N.MR.04.37
MEAP Practice Test 13		
1	C	N.ME.04.04
2	D	N.MR.04.06
3	C	D.AN.05.03
4	B	N.ME.04.04
5	see p. 204	N.ME.04.04
MEAP Practice Test 14		
1	D	N.FL.04.14
2	A	N.FL.04.14
3	C	N.FL.04.34
4	A	N.MR.04.37
5	see p. 204	N.MR.04.37

Answer Key and Correlations

Item	Answer	GLE
MEAP Practice Test 15		
1	B	M.TE.04.05
2	B	M.UN.04.01
3	C	M.TE.04.05
4	C	M.UN.04.01
5	see p. 205	N.MR.04.35
MEAP Practice Test 16		
1	A	M.UN.04.03
2	C	D.RE.04.02
3	C	M.UN.04.03
4	B	M.UN.04.03
5	see p. 205	N.MR.04.37
MEAP Practice Test 17		
1	C	D.RE.04.02
2	C	D.RE.04.02
3	C	D.RE.04.03
4	C	D.RE.04.02
5	see p. 206	D.RE.04.01
MEAP Practice Test 18		
1	D	D.RE.04.01
2	B	D.RE.04.03
3	D	D.RE.04.03
4	B	D.RE.04.03
5	see p. 207	D.RE.04.01
MEAP Practice Test 19		
1	D	M.TE.04.10
2	A	G.GS.04.02
3	B	G.GS.04.01
4	C	G.GS.04.02
5	see p. 207	G.GS.04.01
MEAP Practice Test 20		
1	D	G.TR.04.04
2	B	G.TR.04.04
3	C	G.TR.04.05
4	D	G.TR.04.04
5	see p. 208	G.TR.04.04
MEAP Practice Test 21		
1	D	M.TE.04.06
2	C	M.TE.04.08
3	B	M.TE.04.06
4	D	M.MR.04.24
5	see p. 208	M.TE.04.06

Answer Key and Correlations

Item	Answer	GLE
MEAP Practice Test 22		
1	C	N.ME.04.20
2	D	N.MR.04.26
3	C	N.MR.04.21
4	D	N.MR.04.25
5	see p. 209	N.MR.04.37
MEAP Practice Test 23		
1	B	N.MR.04.37
2	B	N.MR.04.37
3	B	N.MR.04.37
4	D	N.FL.04.28
5	see p. 209	N.MR.04.37
MEAP Practice Test 24		
1	C	N.ME.04.15
2	A	N.ME.04.18
3	A	N.MR.04.37
4	D	N.MR.04.37
5	see p. 210	N.MR.04.37
MEAP Practice Test 25		
1	B	N.MR.04.37
2	C	N.FL.04.32
3	D	N.FL.04.32
4	D	N.FL.04.32
5	see p. 210	N.MR.04.37
MEAP Practice Test 26		
1	D	G.GS.04.02
2	A	N.MR.04.23
3	C	N.PS.04.09
4	C	G.GS.04.02
5	see p. 211	G.SR.04.03
MEAP Practice Test 27		
1	D	G.SR.04.03
2	B	M.TE.04.05
3	B	M.FL.04.34
4	C	N.MR.04.22
5	see p. 212	N.FL.04.32
MEAP Practice Test 28		
1	C	G.GS.04.01
2	B	M.PS.04.11
3	A	N.FL.04.34
4	B	N.MR.04.37
5	see p. 213	N.MR.04.37

SCORING RUBRICS
Practice Tests

Practice Test 1, Item 5

A **4-point** response includes all of the following:
- Indicates correct answers for both questions in the item.
  - o 2 students read 4 books.
  - o Sofia read 7 books.
- Provides a clear explanation of how each answer was derived. For example: I looked at the height of the bar above the number 4. It reaches to the line for the number 2, so 2 students read 4 books. To find how many books Sofia read, I looked at the greatest number of books shown on the graph: 7. One student read 7 books, so Sofia must have read 7 books.

A **3-point** response includes the following:
- Correct answers for both questions in the item
- Explanation that shows good understanding of the questions and how to find the answers, but
- Explanation is missing a step or is otherwise unclear.

A **2-point** response includes the following:
- Correct answer to one question, but not both
- Answer to other question is incorrect, unclear, or missing.
- Explanation shows some understanding of how to interpret bar graphs, but lacks clarity.

A **1-point** response includes the following:
- A partial response on one of the questions; attempts to answer are unclear or only partially correct.
- Explanation exhibits limited understanding of bar graphs.

A **0-point** response shows little or no understanding of the problem. No attempt is made to explain the work and all answers are incorrect.

Practice Test 2, Item 5

A **4-point** response includes all of the following:
- Indicates correct answers for both questions in the item.
  - o Part A: Marquita packs 56 books.
  - o Part B: Marquita packs 23 magazines.
- Provides a clear explanation of how each answer was derived. For example: I know there are 7 bags, and 8 books will be put in each bag. I used multiplication to find the total number of books. $8 \times 7 = 56$. Marquita puts 4 magazines into 2 of the bags; $4 \times 2 = 8$. She puts 3 magazines into 5 of the bags; $3 \times 5 = 15$. $8 + 15 = 23$. Marquita packs 23 magazines in all.

A **3-point** response includes the following:
- Correct answers for both questions in the item
- Explanation that shows good understanding of the questions and how to find the answers, but
- Explanation is missing some steps or is otherwise unclear.

A **2-point** response includes the following:
- Correct answer to one question, but not both
- Answer to other question is incorrect, unclear, or missing.
- Explanation shows some understanding of division and multiplication, but lacks clarity.

A **1-point** response includes the following:
- A partial response on one of the questions; attempts to answer are unclear or only partially correct.
- Explanation exhibits limited understanding of division and/or multiplication.

A **0-point** response shows little or no understanding of the problem. No attempt is made to explain the work and all answers are incorrect.

Practice Test 3, Item 5

A **4-point** response includes all of the following:
- Indicates correct answers for both questions in the item.
  - o Long sides should be labeled 22 feet; short sides should be labeled 19 feet.
  - o 82 feet
- Provides a clear explanation of how the answer was derived. For example: First, I labeled the length and width of the garden. Then I added the lengths of the 4 sides together to find the perimeter of the garden. The total is the number of feet of fencing Mr. Chen needs to buy for the garden: 22 feet + 19 feet + 22 feet + 19 feet = 82 feet.

A **3-point** response includes the following:
- Correct answers for both questions in the item
- Explanation that shows good understanding of the questions and how to find the answers, but
- Explanation is missing some labels or is otherwise unclear.

A **2-point** response includes the following:
- Correct answer to one question, but not both
- Answer to other question is incorrect, unclear, or missing.
- Explanation shows some understanding of perimeter but lacks clarity.

A **1-point** response includes the following:
- A partial response on one of the questions; attempts to answer are unclear or only partially correct.
- Explanation exhibits limited understanding of perimeter.
- Does not explain how to find the perimeter.

A **0-point** response shows little or no understanding of the problem. No attempt is made to explain the work and all answers are incorrect.

Practice Test 4, Item 5

A **4-point** response includes all of the following:
- Indicates correct answer for the question in the item.
  - o Demetrius picked cards with the numbers 3, 5, 7, and 8.
- Provides a clear explanation of how the answer was derived. For example: I listed the numbers between 1 and 12. The greatest even number less than 12 is 10. Since all the odd numbers are less than the even number, the possible odd numbers are 3, 5, 7, and 9. The even number cannot be 4, since there are not 3 odd numbers that are less than 4. The even number must be 8, because 8 is the only other number less than 12 that can be evenly divided by 4. Since the odd numbers are less than 8 but greater than 1, they must be 3, 5, and 7. The cards have the numbers 3, 5, 7, and 8.
- Demonstrates the ability to find numbers that can be divided evenly by 4.
- All work is clearly shown.

A **3-point** response includes the following:
- Correct answer for the question in the item
- Explanation that shows good understanding of the question and how to find the answer, but
- Explanation is missing some steps or is otherwise unclear.

A **2-point** response includes the following:
- Answer to question is only partially correct or unclear.
- Explanation shows some understanding of odd and even numbers but lacks clarity.

A **1-point** response includes the following:
- Attempts to answer are unclear or only partially correct.
- Explanation exhibits limited understanding of odd and even numbers.

A **0-point** response shows little or no understanding of the problem. No attempt is made to explain the work and all answers are incorrect.

Practice Test 5, Item 5

A **4-point** response includes all of the following:
- Indicates correct answer for the question in the item.
  - o   Yes, Tanya has enough money.
- Provides a clear explanation of how the answer was derived. For example: When I round to the nearest dollar, $2.85 rounds to $3, $1.75 rounds to $2, and $0.99 rounds to $1. $3 + $2 + $1 = $6. Tanya has $6.26 altogether because 5 one-dollar bills and 9 quarters are equal to $6.25. Since $6 < $6.25 and all the amounts were rounded up, Tanya has enough money.
- Demonstrates the ability to count money.
- Demonstrates the ability to round to the nearest dollar.

A **3-point** response includes the following:
- Correct answer for the question in the item
- Explanation that shows good understanding of the question and how to find the answer, but
- Explanation is missing some steps or is otherwise unclear.

A **2-point** response includes the following:
- Answer to question is only partially correct or unclear.
- Explanation shows some understanding of rounding but lacks clarity.
- Explanation shows some understanding of counting money but lacks clarity.

A **1-point** response includes the following:
- Attempts to answer are unclear or only partially correct.
- Explanation exhibits limited understanding of rounding and counting money.

A **0-point** response shows little or no understanding of the problem. No attempt is made to explain the work and the answer is incorrect.

Practice Test 6, Item 5

A **4-point** response includes all of the following:
- Indicates correct answers for both questions in the item.
  - o   There are 76 more books in Keisha's school's library than in Dani's.
  - o   723 books in Keisha's school's library; 723 books in Dani's school's library.
- Provides a clear explanation of how each answer was derived. For example: I found the difference by subtracting the smaller number from the larger number. 761 − 685 = 76. To find the number of books in each school's library, I subtracted 38 from 761 to find the number of books in Keisha's school's library. 761 − 38 = 723. I added 38 to 685 to find the number of books in Dani's school's library. 685 + 38 = 723.

A **3-point** response includes the following:
- Correct answers for both questions in the item
- Explanation that shows good understanding of the questions and how to find the answers, but
- Explanation is missing a step or is otherwise unclear.

A **2-point** response includes the following:
- Correct answer to one of the questions, but not both
- Answer to other question is incorrect, unclear, or missing.
- Explanation shows some understanding of addition and subtraction, but lacks clarity.

A **1-point** response includes the following:
- A partial response on one of the questions; attempts to answer are unclear or only partially correct.
- Explanation exhibits limited understanding of addition and subtraction.

A **0-point** response shows little or no understanding of the problem. No attempt is made to explain the work and all answers are incorrect.

Practice Test 7, Item 5

A **4-point** response includes all of the following:
- Indicates correct answers for both questions in the item.
  - o 27 boxes
  - o 14 trips
- Provides a clear explanation of how each answer was derived. For example: I divided 20 by 5. The answer is 4. Andrew needs 4 boxes to pack all the dishes. Then I divided the rest of the 9 items. $43 \div 9 = 4$ R7. Andrew needs 4 boxes for 36 glasses, plus another one for the remaining 7 glasses. $28 \div 5 = 5$ R3 (6 boxes needed for the bowls), $84 \div 7 = 12$ (12 boxes for the books). Then I added to find the total number of boxes he needs. $4 + 5 + 6 + 12 = 27$ boxes. To find the number of trips, I divided the number of boxes (27) by the number of boxes per trip (2). $27 \div 2 = 13$ R1. Andrew needs to make 14 trips to the van.

A **3-point** response includes the following:
- Correct answers for both questions in the item
- Explanation that shows good understanding of the questions and how to find the answers, but
- Explanation is missing a step or is otherwise unclear.

A **2-point** response includes the following:
- Correct answer to one of the questions, but not both
- Answer to other question is incorrect, unclear, or missing.
- Explanation shows some understanding of division with remainders, but lacks clarity.

A **1-point** response includes the following:
- A partial response on one of the questions; attempts to answer are unclear or only partially correct.
- Explanation exhibits limited understanding of division.

A **0-point** response shows little or no understanding of the problem. No attempt is made to explain the work and all answers are incorrect.

Practice Test 8, Item 5

A **4-point** response includes all of the following:
- Indicates correct answers for both questions in the item.
  - o $8p = 56$; $p = 7$; 7 posters; Possible explanation: 56 = total number of photos. p = number of posters Jamie needs. Each poster holds 8 photos, so $8p = 56$; $8p \div 8 = 56 \div 8$; $p = 7$. Jamie needs 7 posters.
  - o Annalisa needs 7 posters. Possible explanation: Since Annalisa has half as many photos as Jamie, I divided to find how many photos Annalisa has. $56 \div 2 = 28$. She puts 4 photos on each poster. $28 \div 4 = 7$. Annalisa needs 7 posters.
- Uses both words and symbols in the explanation.

A **3-point** response includes the following:
- Correct answers for both questions in the item
- Explanation that shows good understanding of the questions and how to find the answers, but
- Explanation is missing some steps or is otherwise unclear.

A **2-point** response includes the following:
- Correct answer to only one of the questions, but not both
- Answer to other question is incorrect, unclear, or missing.
- Explanation shows some understanding of writing and solving an equation, but lacks clarity.

A **1-point** response includes the following:
- A partial response on one of the questions; attempts to answer are unclear or only partially correct.
- Explanation exhibits limited understanding of writing and solving an equation.

A **0-point** response shows little or no understanding of the problem. No attempt is made to explain the work and all answers are incorrect.

Practice Test 9, Item 5

A **4-point** response includes all of the following:
- Indicates correct answer for both parts of the question in the item.
  - o Alyssa won 16 ribbons. Mario won 8 ribbons.
  - o Rick
- Provides a clear explanation of how the answer was derived. For example: I used Guess-and-Check to find the correct numbers. I looked for numbers that had a sum of 24 with one number twice as great as the other. First guess: Alyssa wins 14 ribbons. Mario wins 10 ribbons. $14 + 10 = 24$; $2 \times 10 \neq 14$. Second guess: Alyssa wins 15 ribbons. Mario wins 9 ribbons. $15 + 9 = 24$; $2 \times 9 \neq 15$. Third guess: Alyssa wins 16 ribbons. Mario wins 8 ribbons. $16 + 8 = 24$; $2 \times 8 = 16$. This guess was correct. Rick won 10 more ribbons than Mario. $8 + 10 = 18$. So, Rick won 18 ribbons. Since $18 > 16$, Rick won more ribbons than Alyssa.
- Demonstrates the ability to add and multiply to find the correct answer

A **3-point** response includes the following:
- Correct answer for both questions in the item
- Explanation that shows good understanding of the questions and how to find the answers, but
- Explanation is missing some steps or is otherwise unclear

A **2-point** response includes the following:
- Correct answer to one of the questions, but not both
- Answer to the other question is incorrect, unclear, or missing.
- Explanation shows some understanding of addition and multiplication but lacks clarity.

A **1-point** response includes the following:
- Attempts to answer are unclear or only partially correct.
- Explanation exhibits limited understanding of addition and multiplication

A **0-point** response shows little or no understanding of the problem. No attempt is made to explain the work and the answer is incorrect.

Practice Test 10, Item 5

A **4-point** response includes all of the following:
- Indicates correct answer for the question in the item.
  - o They need to collect 1,240 bottles.
- Provides a clear explanation of how the answer was derived. For example: First I multiplied to find the cost of 9 T-shirts. $9 \times \$16.87 = \$61.83$. I rounded $61.83 to $62. There are 20 nickels in a dollar. So, I multiplied $\$62 \times 20 = 1,240$ nickels. Rosa and her teammates need about 1,240 nickels or 1,240 bottles to buy the T-shirts.
- All work is clearly shown.

A **3-point** response includes the following:
- Correct answer for the question in the item
- Explanation that shows good understanding of the question and how to find the answer, but
- Explanation is missing some steps or is otherwise unclear.

A **2-point** response includes the following:
- Answer to question is only partially correct or unclear.
- Explanation shows some understanding of multiplication and estimation but lacks clarity.
- Does not explain estimation clearly.

A **1-point** response includes the following:
- Attempts to answer are unclear or only partially correct.
- Explanation exhibits limited understanding of multiplication and estimation.
- Does not explain how to use estimation to find out if the answer is reasonable.

A **0-point** response shows little or no understanding of the problem. No attempt is made to explain the work and the answer is incorrect.

Practice Test 11, Item 5

A **4-point** response includes all of the following:
- Indicates correct answer for the question in the item.
  - o 500 boxes
  - o 14 layers
- Provides a clear explanation of how each answer was derived. For example: To find how many boxes, I divided 5,000 by 10 and got 500. I divided 84 by 6 to get 14 layers. To check my answers: $500 \times 10 = 5,000$ and $14 \times 6 = 84$.

A **3-point** response includes the following:
- Correct answer for the questions in the item
- Explanation that shows good understanding of the questions and how to find the answers, but
- Explanation is missing some steps or is otherwise unclear.

A **2-point** response includes the following:
- Answer to questions is only partially correct or unclear.
- Explanation shows some understanding of division but lacks clarity.

A **1-point** response includes the following:
- Attempts to answer are unclear or only partially correct.
- Explanation exhibits limited understanding of division.

A **0-point** response shows little or no understanding of the problem. No attempt is made to explain the work and the answer is incorrect.

Practice Test 12, Item 5

A **4-point** response includes all of the following:
- Indicates correct answer for the questions in the item
  - o 102 jeans
  - o 36 T-shirts
- Provides a clear explanation of how each answer was derived. For example: I divided 918 by 9 to get 102. So, there are 102 jeans on each shelf. I divided 216 by 6 to get 36. So, there are 36 T-shirts on each shelf. I checked the answer using multiplication. $102 \times 9 = 918$. $36 \times 6 = 216$.

A **3-point** response includes the following:
- Correct answer for both questions in the item
- Explanation that shows good understanding of the questions and how to find the answers, but
- Explanation is missing some steps or is otherwise unclear.

A **2-point** response includes the following:
- Answers to the questions are only partially correct or unclear.
- Explanation shows some understanding of division and problem solving but lacks clarity

A **1-point** response includes the following:
- Attempts to answer are unclear or only partially correct.
- Explanation exhibits limited understanding of division and problem solving.

A **0-point** response shows little or no understanding of the problem. No attempt is made to explain the work and the answer is incorrect.

Practice Test 13, Item 5

A **4-point** response includes all of the following:
- Indicates correct answer for the question in the item.
  - o   No, Rodney is not right.
- Provides a clear explanation of how the answer was derived. For example: I created a list of the first five multiples of 5 (5, 10, 15, 20, 25) and the first five multiples of ten (10, 20, 30, 40, 50). I realized that every multiple of 5 is not a multiple of 10. For example, 15 is not a multiple of 10.
- Demonstrates an understanding of multiples.

A **3-point** response includes the following:
- Correct answer for the question in the item
- Explanation that shows good understanding of the question and how to find the answer, but
- Explanation is missing some steps or is otherwise unclear.

A **2-point** response includes the following:
- Answer to question is only partially correct or unclear.
- Explanation shows some understanding of multiples but lacks clarity.

A **1-point** response includes the following:
- Explanation exhibits limited understanding of multiples.

A **0-point** response shows little or no understanding of the problem. No attempt is made to explain the work and the answer is incorrect.

Practice Test 14, Item 5

A **4-point** response includes all of the following:
- Indicates correct answer for the questions in the item.
  - o   Adult admission is $9.00.
  - o   6 children.
- Provides a clear explanation of how the answers were derived. For example: I multiplied to find the cost of admission for the children. $4 \times \$2 = \$8$. Then I subtracted the children's admission from the total admission to find the admission for 2 adults. $\$26 - \$8 = \$18$. I divided by 2 to find the admission for 1 adult. $\$18 \div 2 = \$9$. To find out how many children could go with 3 adults for $40, I first multiplied 3 by $9 and got $27. $\$40 - \$27 = \$13$. $\$13 \div \$2 = 6$ R1. 6 children could go.
- Demonstrates an understanding of multiplication and division.

A **3-point** response includes the following:
- Correct answers for the questions in the item
- Explanation that shows good understanding of the questions and how to find the answers, but
- Explanation is missing some steps or is otherwise unclear.

A **2-point** response includes the following:
- Answers to questions are only partially correct or unclear.
- Explanation shows some understanding of problem solving, multiplication, and division but lacks clarity.

A **1-point** response includes the following:
- Attempts to answer are unclear or only partially correct.
- Explanation exhibits limited understanding of problem solving, multiplication, and division.

A **0-point** response shows little or no understanding of the problem. No attempt is made to explain the work and the answer is incorrect.

Practice Test 15, Item 5

A **4-point** response includes all of the following:
- Indicates correct answers for both questions in the item.
  - o No, Yuki does not use enough broth.
  - o 2 cups of rice.
- Provides a clear explanation of how each answer was derived. For example: There are 8 cups in half a gallon. So, Yuki does not use enough broth. The recipe calls for 8 cups of broth for 4 cups of rice. Yuki uses 2 pints of broth, which equals 4 cups. So, she can cook 2 cups of rice.
- All work is clearly shown

A **3-point** response includes the following:
- Correct answers for both questions in the item
- Explanation that shows good understanding of the questions and how to find the answers, but
- Explanation is missing a step or is otherwise unclear.

A **2-point** response includes the following:
- Correct answer to one of the questions, but not both
- Answer to other question is incorrect, unclear, or missing.
- Explanation shows some understanding of problem solving and measurement, but lacks clarity.

A **1-point** response includes the following:
- A partial response on the questions; attempts to answer are unclear or only partially correct.
- Explanation exhibits limited understanding of problem solving and measurement.

A **0-point** response shows little or no understanding of the problem. No attempt is made to explain the work and all answers are incorrect.

Practice Test 16, Item 5

A **4-point** response includes all of the following:
- Indicates correct answer for both parts of the question in the item.
  - o 38 oranges
  - o 23 tangerines
- Provides a clear explanation of how the answer was derived. For example: I used the Guess-and-Check strategy to find the answer. First I guessed 35 oranges and 26 tangerines, for a total of 61. That would make only 9 more oranges than tangerines, which is not enough oranges. Then I guessed 40 oranges and 21 tangerines. That would make 19 more oranges than tangerines, which is too many oranges. Finally I tried 38 oranges and 23 tangerines. This works because 38 + 23 = 61, and there are 15 more oranges than tangerines.
- Demonstrates the ability to use a problem solving strategy to find the correct answer.

A **3-point** response includes the following:
- Correct answer for both parts of the question in the item
- Explanation that shows good understanding of the question and how to find the answer, but
- Explanation is missing some steps or is otherwise unclear.

A **2-point** response includes the following:
- Correct answer to only part of the questions, but not both
- Answer to the other part is incorrect, unclear, or missing.
- Explanation shows some understanding of problem solving but lacks clarity.

A **1-point** response includes the following:
- Attempts to answer are unclear or only partially correct.
- Explanation exhibits limited understanding of problem solving.

A **0-point** response shows little or no understanding of the problem. No attempt is made to explain the work and the answer is incorrect.

Practice Test 17, Item 5

A **4-point** response includes all of the following:
- Indicates correct answer for both parts of the question in the item.
  - o

Game	Points Scored
1	43
2	48
3	36
4	41
5	45
6	38
7	54
8	46
9	40
10	51

  - o The range of the basketball scores is 18.
- Provides a clear explanation of how the range was derived. For example: I subtracted the least score in the table from the greatest score. $54 - 36 = 18$. The range of the basketball scores is 18.
- The table is labeled accurately

A **3-point** response includes the following:
- Correct answer for both parts of the question in the item
- Explanation that shows good understanding of the question and how to find the answer, but
- Table is missing some labels or is otherwise unclear.

A **2-point** response includes the following:
- Correct answer to only one part of the question
- Answer to the other part is incorrect, unclear, or missing.
- Explanation shows some understanding of how to find the range of data but lacks clarity.

A **1-point** response includes the following:
- Attempts to answer are unclear or only partially correct.
- Explanation exhibits limited understanding of finding the range of data.

A **0-point** response shows little or no understanding of the problem. No attempt is made to explain the work and the answer is incorrect.

Practice Test 18, Item 5

A **4-point** response includes all of the following:
- Indicates correct answer for both parts of the question in the item.
  - o

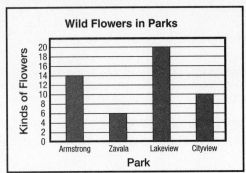

  - o 14 more kinds of wild flowers grow in Lakeview Park than in Zavala Park.
- The graph is titled, includes labels, and has an appropriate scale.
- All the data is graphed accurately.

A **3-point** response includes the following:
- Correct answer for both parts of the question in the item
- Explanation that shows good understanding of the question and how to find the answer, but
- Graph is missing some labels or is otherwise unclear.

A **2-point** response includes the following:
- Correct answer to only one part of the question, but not both
- Answer to the other part is incorrect, unclear, or missing.
- Explanation shows some understanding of bar graphs but lacks clarity.

A **1-point** response includes the following:
- Attempts to answer are unclear or only partially correct.
- Explanation exhibits limited understanding of bar graphs.

A **0-point** response shows little or no understanding of the problem. No attempt is made to explain the work and the answer is incorrect.

Practice Test 19, Item 5

A **4-point** response includes all of the following:
- Indicates correct answer for the question in the item.
  - o No, Quincy is not correct.
- Provides a clear explanation of how the answer was derived. For example: Quincy is incorrect because quadrilaterals may or may not have perpendicular sides.
- Includes drawings to demonstrate quadrilaterals with sides that are perpendicular and not perpendicular.

A **3-point** response includes the following:
- Correct answer for the question in the item
- Explanation that shows good understanding of the question and how to find the answer, but
- Explanation is missing some drawings or is otherwise unclear.

A **2-point** response includes the following:
- Answer to question is only partially correct or unclear.
- Explanation shows some understanding of quadrilaterals and perpendicular lines but lacks clarity.

A **1-point** response includes the following:
- Attempts to answer are unclear or only partially correct.
- Explanation exhibits limited understanding of quadrilaterals and perpendicular lines.

A **0-point** response shows little or no understanding of the problem. No attempt is made to explain the work and the answer is incorrect.

Practice Test 20, Item 5

A **4-point** response includes all of the following:
- Indicates correct answers for each part of the question in the item.
  - o yes
  - o The letter O or the letter M with a line of symmetry drawn through the letter.
    Possible answers:

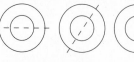

  - o Check student work on their initials.
- Provides a clear explanation of how the answer to the first part of the question was derived. For example: Omar is correct because if the letters were cut out, each could be folded in half so that the two parts would match exactly.

A **3-point** response includes the following:
- Correct answers for all three parts of the question.
- Explanation that shows good understanding of the question and how to find the answer, but
- Explanation is unclear

A **2-point** response includes the following:
- Correct answer to one part of the question
- Answer to other parts is incorrect, unclear, or missing.
- Explanation shows some understanding of line symmetry but lacks clarity.

A **1-point** response includes the following:
- A partial response on one part of the question; attempts to answer are unclear or only partially correct.
- Explanation exhibits limited understanding of line symmetry.

A **0-point** response shows little or no understanding of the problem. No attempt is made to explain the work and all answers are incorrect.

Practice Test 21, Item 5

A **4-point** response includes all of the following:
- Indicates correct answers for both questions in the item.
  - o 162 square feet
  - o 54 feet of fencing
- Provides a clear explanation of how each answer was derived. For example: To find how many square feet of ground the garden covers, I needed to find the area. I used the formula for the area of a rectangle: $A = l \times w$; $A = 18$ feet $\times 9$ feet; $A = 162$ square feet. To find how much fencing is needed to go around the garden, I needed to find the perimeter. I used the formula for the perimeter of a rectangle: $P = (2 \times l) + (2 \times w)$. $P = (2 \times 18$ feet$) + (2 \times 9$ feet$)$; $P = 36$ feet $+ 18$ feet; $P = 54$ feet

A **3-point** response includes the following:
- Correct answers for both questions in the item
- Explanation that shows good understanding of the questions and how to find the answers, but
- Explanation is unclear.

A **2-point** response includes the following:
- Correct answer to one question, but not both
- Answer to other question is incorrect, unclear, or missing.
- Explanation shows some understanding of area and perimeter but lacks clarity.

A **1-point** response includes the following:
- A partial response on one of the questions; attempts to answer are unclear or only partially correct.
- Explanation exhibits limited understanding of area and perimeter.

A **0-point** response shows little or no understanding of the problem. No attempt is made to explain the work and all answers are incorrect.

Practice Test 22, Item 5

A **4-point** response includes all of the following:
- Indicates correct answer for the question in the item.
  - o Molly brings 45 muffins.
- Provides a clear explanation of how the answer was derived. For example: I drew a rectangle to represent all the muffins. Then I separated it into 9 equal parts. I know that $\frac{1}{3} = \frac{3}{9}$, so $\frac{3}{9}$ of the muffins are cranberry. $\frac{4}{9}$ of the muffins are blueberry. 10 apple muffins are $\frac{2}{9}$ of all the muffins. So each $\frac{1}{9}$ equals 5 muffins. $9 \times 5 = 45$. Molly brings 45 muffins.

- Includes a drawing to illustrate the solution.

A **3-point** response includes the following:
- Correct answer for the question in the item
- Explanation that shows good understanding of the question and how to find the answer, but
- The drawing is missing or is unclear.

A **2-point** response includes the following:
- Answer to question is only partially correct or unclear.
- Explanation shows some understanding of a problem solving strategy and fraction concepts but lacks clarity.

A **1-point** response includes the following:
- Attempts to answer are unclear or only partially correct.
- Explanation exhibits limited understanding of problem solving and fractions.

A **0-point** response shows little or no understanding of the problem. No attempt is made to explain the work and the answer is incorrect.

Practice Test 23, Item 5

A **4-point** response includes all of the following:
- Indicates correct answers for the questions in the item.
  - o Janet saves $\frac{1}{3}$ of her allowance each month.
  - o Janet spends $15 on books, $15 on music, and $30 on food. She saves $30 each month.
- Provides a clear explanation of how the answer was derived. For example: I added $\frac{1}{6} + \frac{1}{6} + \frac{1}{3} = \frac{2}{3}$. One whole minus $\frac{2}{3}$ is $\frac{1}{3}$. So Janet saved $\frac{1}{3}$ of her allowance. To find out how much she spends on books I multiplied $\frac{1}{6} \times \$90 = \$15$. Janet spends the same amount ($\frac{1}{6}$) on music. She spends $\frac{1}{3}$ on food so I multiplied. $\frac{1}{3} \times \$90 = 30$. If Janet spends $15 + $15 + $30 = $60 then she saves $30 because $90 − $60 = $30.
- All work is clearly shown.

A **3-point** response includes the following:
- Correct answer for the question in the item
- Explanation that shows good understanding of the question and how to find the answer, but
- Shown work is missing or is unclear.

A **2-point** response includes the following:
- Correct answer to only one question in the item.
- Explanation shows some understanding of fractions, but lacks clarity.

A **1-point** response includes the following:
- Attempts to answer are unclear or only partially correct.
- Explanation exhibits limited understanding of fractions.

A **0-point** response shows little or no understanding of the problem. No attempt is made to explain the work and the answer is incorrect.

Practice Test 24, Item 5

A **4-point** response includes all of the following:
- Indicates correct answer for the question in the item.
  - o Six caps will cost $58.50.
- Provides a clear explanation of how the answer was derived. For example: First I looked for a pattern in the table. The pattern is to add $12.50 to the first amount and $2.00 less to each amount after that. I continued the pattern to find the answer. 4 caps cost $47.50. $47.50 + $6.50 = $54.00, so 5 caps cost $54.00. $54.00 + $4.50 = $58.50, so 6 caps cost $58.50.
- All work is clearly shown.

A **3-point** response includes the following:
- Correct answer for the question in the item
- Explanation that shows good understanding of the question and how to find the answer, but
- Shown work is missing or is unclear.

A **2-point** response includes the following:
- Answer to question is only partially correct or unclear.
- Explanation shows some understanding of a problem solving strategy but lacks clarity.

A **1-point** response includes the following:
- Attempts to answer are unclear or only partially correct.
- Explanation exhibits limited understanding of problem solving.

A **0-point** response shows little or no understanding of the problem. No attempt is made to explain the work and the answer is incorrect.

Practice Test 25, Item 5

A **4-point** response includes all of the following:
- Indicates correct answer for the question in the item.
  - o 0.41 mile
  - o 5.04 miles
- Provides a clear explanation of how the answer was derived. For example: First I looked in the table to find the length of the longest trail. Basin Creek Trail is 3.3 miles long. Then I looked in the table to find the length of the shortest trail. Bluff Ridge Trail is 2.89 miles long. Finally, I subtracted to find the difference: 3.3 − 2.89 = 0.41. To find how far Mike hiked it both days I added 0.84 + 4.2 = 5.04. He hiked 5.04 miles.

A **3-point** response includes the following:
- Correct answer for both questions in the item
- Explanation that shows good understanding of the questions and how to find the answers, but
- Explanation is missing some steps or is otherwise unclear.

A **2-point** response includes the following:
- Answers to questions are only partially correct or unclear.
- Explanation shows some understanding of interpreting tables and decimal operations, but lacks clarity.

A **1-point** response includes the following:
- Attempts to answer are unclear or only partially correct.
- Explanation exhibits limited understanding of interpreting tables and decimal operations.

A **0-point** response shows little or no understanding of the problem. No attempt is made to explain the work and the answer is incorrect.

Practice Test 26, Item 5

A **4-point** response includes all of the following:
- Indicates correct answers for both parts of the question.
  - o Similarities:
    Both have at least one square face.
    Both are three-dimensional.
    All faces are flat (no curved surfaces).

  - o Differences:
    Different number of faces, edges, and vertices.
    Four faces meet at one vertex.
    You can easily stack cubes.

A **3-point** response includes the following:
- Correct answers for both parts of the question
- Explanation that shows good understanding of the question and how to find the answer, but
- Explanation is missing a step or is otherwise unclear.

A **2-point** response includes the following:
- Correct answer to only one part, but not both
- Answer to other part is incorrect, unclear, or missing.
- Explanation shows some understanding of solids, but lacks clarity.

A **1-point** response includes the following:
- A partial response on one part of the question; attempts to answer are unclear or only partially correct.
- Explanation exhibits limited understanding of solids.

A **0-point** response shows little or no understanding of the problem. No attempt is made to explain the work and all answers are incorrect.

Practice Test 27, Item 5

A **4-point** response includes all of the following:
- Indicates correct answers for both questions in the item.
  - o Chris H., Malcolm R., and Liang T. qualify for the event finals.
  - o 5.11 seconds
- Provides a clear explanation of how the answers were derived. For example: I ordered all the times in the table to find the 3 fastest times. The 3 swimmers with lowest times were Chris H., Malcolm R., and Liang T. I found the fastest swimmer (Chris H.) and the slowest swimmer (Jan T.). I used subtraction to find the difference between their times. $51.34 - 46.23 = 5.11$ seconds.
- Data from the table is plotted accurately on the grid.

A **3-point** response includes the following:
- Correct answers for both questions in the item
- Explanation that shows good understanding of the questions and how to find the answers, but
- Explanation is missing a step or is otherwise unclear.

A **2-point** response includes the following:
- Correct answer to only one of the questions, but not both
- Answer to other part is incorrect, unclear, or missing.
- Explanation shows some understanding of decimal place value and operations, but lacks clarity.

A **1-point** response includes the following:
- A partial response on one of the questions; attempts to answer are unclear or only partially correct.
- Explanation exhibits limited understanding of decimal place value and operations.

A **0-point** response shows little or no understanding of the problem. No attempt is made to explain the work and all answers are incorrect.

Practice Test 28, Item 5

A **4-point** response includes all of the following:
- Indicates correct answer for the question in the item.
  - o There are 43 baseball cards on each shelf.
  - o Bryan needs 13 shelves
- Provides a clear explanation of how each answer was derived. For example: First I multiplied the number of boxes, 4, by the number of baseball cards in each box, 86, to find the total number of baseball cards. $4 \times 86 = 344$. There are a total of 344 baseball cards. Then I divided the total number of baseball cards, 344, by the number of shelves, 8, to find the number of baseball cards on each shelf. $344 \div 8 = 43$. There are 43 baseball cards on each shelf.

  First I added to find how many more baseball cards Bryan found. $72 + 68 + 75 = 215$. Then I divided to see how many more shelves Bryan needs if he continues to put 43 cards on each shelf. $215 \div 43 = 5$. Bryan will need 5 more shelves in addition to the 8 he already has. $5 + 8 = 13$. Bryan needs 13 shelves altogether.
- All work is clearly shown.

A **3-point** response includes the following:
- Correct answer for both questions in the item
- Explanation that shows good understanding of the questions and how to find the answers, but
- Explanation is missing some steps or is otherwise unclear.

A **2-point** response includes the following:
- Answer to questions are only partially correct or unclear.
- Explanation shows some understanding of using multiplication and division, but lacks clarity.

A **1-point** response includes the following:
- Attempts to answer are unclear or only partially correct.
- Explanation exhibits limited understanding of using multiplication and division.

A **0-point** response shows little or no understanding of the problem. No attempt is made to explain the work and the answer is incorrect.

Answer Sheet

Name _____ Date _____

Guided Practice _____	**Practice Test** _____

Guided Practice _____

1. (A) (B) (C) (D)

2. (A) (B) (C) (D)

3. (A) (B) (C) (D)

4. (A) (B) (C) (D)

5.

Practice Test _____

1. (A) (B) (C) (D)

2. (A) (B) (C) (D)

3. (A) (B) (C) (D)

4. (A) (B) (C) (D)

5.